Digital Predator: A Guide to Modern Threat Hunting

Tatsuki Yosuke

Tatsuki Yosuke is a seasoned cybersecurity expert and threat hunting specialist with over a decade of experience in the field. With a strong foundation in computer science and a passion for protecting digital assets, Tatsuki has dedicated his career to unraveling the complexities of modern cyber threats. He has worked with various organizations, from startups to Fortune 500 companies, helping them develop robust security postures and effective threat-hunting strategies.

Throughout his career, Tatsuki has been at the forefront of evolving cybersecurity practices, witnessing firsthand the shift from reactive defense to proactive threat hunting. His expertise encompasses a wide range of topics, including threat intelligence, incident response, and advanced analytics, allowing him to approach cybersecurity challenges from multiple angles. As a regular speaker at cybersecurity conferences and a contributor to industry publications, Tatsuki is committed to sharing knowledge and best practices with the broader security community.

In "**Digital Predator: A Guide to Modern Threat Hunting**," Tatsuki combines his hands-on experience and deep understanding of the threat landscape to provide readers with practical insights and actionable strategies. This book serves as a comprehensive resource for cybersecurity professionals, equipping them with the tools and knowledge needed to effectively hunt down and mitigate threats in an ever-evolving digital environment.

Outside of his professional endeavors, Tatsuki is an avid researcher, always exploring new technologies and methodologies in the field. He believes that continuous learning is vital in cybersecurity, where threats are constantly changing, and the landscape is forever shifting. When he's not hunting digital predators, Tatsuki enjoys hiking, reading about ancient history, and mentoring the next generation of cybersecurity professionals.

In an age where digital landscapes are continuously evolving, the threats that lurk within them are becoming increasingly sophisticated. Cybercriminals, state-sponsored actors, and hacktivists are constantly devising new strategies to exploit vulnerabilities, targeting organizations of all sizes. To combat these threats effectively, the cybersecurity landscape has shifted from reactive measures to proactive strategies—enter threat hunting.

"Digital Predator: A Guide to Modern Threat Hunting" is designed to equip cybersecurity professionals with the knowledge and tools necessary to anticipate, detect, and neutralize threats before they can inflict harm. This book delves into the essential components of modern threat hunting, offering practical insights and actionable strategies for building and maintaining a successful threat hunting program.

Chapter 1: Introduction to Threat Hunting

This chapter provides an overview of threat hunting, tracing its origins and explaining its significance in today's cybersecurity landscape. Readers will learn the key roles and responsibilities involved in effective threat hunting.

Chapter 2: Understanding the Cyber Kill Chain

Here, we break down the cyber kill chain model, which outlines the stages of an attack. This chapter emphasizes the importance of understanding each phase and how disrupting the kill chain can thwart potential breaches.

Chapter 3: The Threat Landscape Today

This chapter analyzes current trends in cyber threats, including high-profile attacks and the evolving tactics of threat actors. It offers insights into the types of threats organizations face and how to prepare for them.

Chapter 4: Setting Up a Threat Hunting Program

Establishing a threat hunting program requires careful planning. This chapter guides readers through identifying organizational needs, creating a framework, and fostering a culture of security awareness.

Chapter 5: Data Collection and Analysis

Data is at the heart of threat hunting. This chapter discusses effective data sources, visualization tools, and techniques for anomaly detection, ensuring that readers can analyze data efficiently.

Chapter 6: Threat Intelligence in Hunting

Understanding and integrating threat intelligence is crucial for effective hunting. This chapter covers the different types of intelligence, evaluating sources, and the importance of collaboration in threat intelligence sharing.

Chapter 7: Developing Hypotheses and Hunt Techniques

Hypothesis-driven hunting is the focus of this chapter, emphasizing the importance of formulating hypotheses based on threat intelligence. Readers will explore common hunting techniques, including behavioral analysis and signature-based detection.

Chapter 8: Incident Response and Collaboration

This chapter outlines the incident response process and best practices for collaboration among teams during a cybersecurity incident. It highlights the significance of learning from past incidents to improve future responses.

Chapter 9: Case Studies in Threat Hunting

Real-world examples illustrate the practical application of threat hunting strategies. This chapter analyzes successful operations and lessons learned from notable cybersecurity breaches.

Chapter 10: Measuring Success in Threat Hunting

Establishing metrics is essential for evaluating the effectiveness of a threat hunting program. This chapter discusses key performance indicators, tools for tracking performance, and how to report findings to stakeholders.

Chapter 11: Future of Threat Hunting

Looking ahead, this chapter explores predictions for the next generation of threats and the role of automation in threat hunting. It emphasizes the importance of adaptability in a rapidly changing cyber landscape.

Chapter 12: Resources for Threat Hunters

The final chapter provides readers with a curated list of essential tools, software, and educational resources. It also highlights networking opportunities within the cybersecurity community.

As we journey through this book, you will gain a comprehensive understanding of the methodologies, tools, and techniques that are essential for modern threat hunting. Whether you are a seasoned professional or just starting in the field, "Digital Predator" aims to empower you to become an effective defender in the ever-changing realm of cybersecurity.

Chapter 1: Introduction to Threat Hunting

In this chapter, we will embark on a journey to understand the foundational concepts of threat hunting, a proactive approach that goes beyond traditional cybersecurity measures. We will explore the origins of threat hunting, tracing its evolution alongside the increasingly sophisticated tactics employed by cyber adversaries. By differentiating threat hunting from reactive security practices, we will highlight its significance in today's digital landscape. Additionally, we will outline the key roles and responsibilities that make up a successful threat hunting team, setting the stage for the deeper insights and strategies to come in the subsequent chapters. As we delve into this dynamic discipline, you will gain a clearer understanding of why threat hunting is essential for safeguarding modern organizations against the myriad of digital threats they face.

1.1 The Origins of Threat Hunting

Threat hunting, as a proactive cybersecurity practice, has emerged as a critical component of modern information security strategies. To fully appreciate its significance in today's threat landscape, it is essential to explore the origins of threat hunting, tracing its evolution from traditional cybersecurity measures to the advanced methodologies employed by security professionals today. This exploration will encompass the historical context of cyber threats, the limitations of conventional security approaches, and the factors that catalyzed the development of threat hunting as a distinct discipline.

The Early Days of Cybersecurity

The roots of threat hunting can be traced back to the early days of computing, when cybersecurity was primarily focused on perimeter defenses and reactive measures. In the 1980s and 1990s, the concept of computer security revolved around preventing unauthorized access to systems and data through firewalls, antivirus software, and basic intrusion detection systems (IDS). Organizations relied heavily on these tools to create a security perimeter, believing that if they could keep threats out, their systems would remain secure.

However, as technology evolved, so did the tactics employed by cybercriminals. The rise of the internet in the late 1990s and early 2000s led to an exponential increase in connectivity and, consequently, vulnerabilities. The traditional focus on perimeter security proved inadequate against more sophisticated attacks, such as insider threats, advanced persistent threats (APTs), and zero-day exploits. The understanding began to shift: threats could originate from within the organization or take advantage of weaknesses in existing defenses.

The Limitations of Reactive Security

By the mid-2000s, organizations started to recognize the limitations of reactive security measures. The proliferation of malware, phishing attacks, and targeted cyber espionage prompted a reassessment of security strategies. Organizations that had invested heavily in firewalls and antivirus solutions found themselves facing data breaches and significant financial losses despite their preventive measures. The reality became clear: simply deploying tools was not enough; proactive measures were necessary to identify and mitigate threats before they could cause harm.

The traditional incident response model, which relied heavily on detecting and responding to security incidents after they occurred, proved inadequate for the growing complexity of cyber threats. Many incidents went unnoticed for extended periods, allowing attackers to move laterally within networks, escalate privileges, and extract sensitive information without detection. The need for a more proactive approach to security led to the birth of threat hunting.

The Emergence of Threat Hunting

Threat hunting emerged as a response to the increasing complexity and persistence of cyber threats. It shifted the focus from merely defending against attacks to actively seeking out threats that had already breached the perimeter defenses. The practice of threat hunting is built on the understanding that attackers are often already inside the network, operating stealthily and evading detection.

The formalization of threat hunting as a distinct discipline can be traced to the work of pioneering cybersecurity professionals and organizations that recognized the importance of proactive detection. Early adopters began to leverage threat intelligence, behavioral analytics, and advanced analytics tools to identify anomalous activity within their networks. This marked a significant shift in cybersecurity philosophy, emphasizing the need for continuous monitoring and analysis.

One of the seminal moments in the evolution of threat hunting was the publication of the "Cyber Kill Chain" model by Lockheed Martin in 2011. This framework outlined the stages of a cyber attack, from initial reconnaissance to exfiltration of data, and provided a roadmap for organizations to disrupt attacks at various phases. The Kill Chain model underscored the need for proactive measures and became a foundational concept for threat hunters, guiding their efforts to identify and mitigate threats.

The Role of Threat Intelligence

The rise of threat intelligence also played a crucial role in the origins of threat hunting. As cyber threats became more sophisticated, the need for timely and actionable intelligence became paramount. Organizations began to gather threat intelligence from various sources, including government agencies, industry groups, and cybersecurity vendors. This intelligence provided insights into emerging threats, attack vectors, and the tactics used by threat actors.

Threat intelligence empowered threat hunters to craft hypotheses about potential threats based on observed patterns and behaviors. By integrating threat intelligence with internal security data, organizations could develop a more comprehensive understanding of their threat landscape. This approach not only enhanced the ability to detect threats but also informed incident response efforts by providing context for security incidents.

The Evolution of Methodologies

As threat hunting matured as a practice, various methodologies and frameworks began to emerge. Organizations started to develop structured hunting processes, often based on the principles of hypothesis-driven hunting. This approach emphasizes the formulation of testable hypotheses about potential threats, enabling hunters to focus their efforts on specific areas of concern. By leveraging data analysis and threat intelligence, threat hunters could investigate anomalies and validate their hypotheses.

One notable development in the field of threat hunting is the adoption of frameworks like MITRE ATT&CK. This knowledge base categorizes the tactics, techniques, and procedures (TTPs) used by adversaries, providing a standardized reference for threat hunters. By aligning their hunting efforts with the ATT&CK framework, organizations can enhance their detection capabilities and ensure they are addressing relevant threats.

The Current State of Threat Hunting

Today, threat hunting has evolved into a sophisticated discipline that combines human expertise with advanced technologies. Organizations are increasingly recognizing the value of threat hunting as part of their overall security strategy. The integration of machine learning and artificial intelligence into threat hunting processes has further enhanced the ability to analyze vast amounts of data and identify patterns indicative of malicious activity.

Furthermore, the ongoing evolution of cyber threats continues to drive the development of threat hunting practices. As cybercriminals adopt new tactics and technologies, threat hunters must remain agile and adaptable, continuously refining their methodologies to stay ahead of evolving threats.

The origins of threat hunting can be traced back to the recognition of the limitations of traditional cybersecurity approaches in the face of increasingly sophisticated threats. As organizations transitioned from reactive security measures to proactive threat hunting, they embraced the necessity of actively seeking out threats within their networks. The development of key frameworks, the integration of threat intelligence, and the evolution of methodologies have all contributed to the establishment of threat hunting as a critical component of modern cybersecurity practices.

As we continue to navigate an ever-changing threat landscape, the importance of threat hunting will only grow. By understanding its origins and the factors that have shaped its evolution, cybersecurity professionals can better appreciate the value of threat hunting in protecting their organizations against the digital predators that threaten their assets and operations. Threat hunting is not just a practice; it is a mindset—one that embraces curiosity, vigilance, and a proactive approach to safeguarding our digital environments.

1.2 Differentiating Threat Hunting from Traditional Security Measures

In the realm of cybersecurity, the evolving landscape of threats has prompted a reassessment of traditional security measures and the emergence of more proactive strategies, such as threat hunting. Understanding the distinctions between these approaches is crucial for organizations aiming to fortify their defenses against sophisticated cyber threats. This chapter will explore the key differences between threat hunting and traditional security measures, including their methodologies, objectives, and roles in an organization's overall cybersecurity posture.

Traditional Security Measures

Traditional security measures have historically focused on establishing a perimeter defense to protect information systems and networks from external threats. The foundation of these measures is built upon several core components:

Preventive Controls: Traditional security strategies prioritize preventive controls such as firewalls, intrusion detection systems (IDS), antivirus software, and access controls. These tools aim to create barriers that block unauthorized access and mitigate the risk of malware infections. Organizations have relied heavily on these preventive measures to maintain a secure environment.

Reactive Approach: Traditional security often operates on a reactive basis, meaning that it focuses on responding to incidents after they occur. Security teams analyze alerts generated by their security tools, investigate potential breaches, and deploy patches or remediations after vulnerabilities are exploited. This approach can lead to significant delays in detecting and responding to active threats.

Perimeter Defense: Traditional security emphasizes the concept of a defined perimeter around the organization's network, which separates trusted internal resources from untrusted external entities. This model assumes that threats originate outside the network, and once the perimeter is secure, the internal environment is considered safe. However, this perspective is increasingly inadequate as cyber threats have evolved to target both external and internal vectors.

Limited Visibility: While traditional security measures can provide a certain level of visibility into network activity, they often lack the depth required to detect sophisticated attacks. Security teams may struggle to correlate data from disparate tools, leading to blind spots and delayed incident detection. Many traditional security solutions focus on known threats and signature-based detection, making them less effective against zero-day exploits and advanced persistent threats (APTs).

Threat Hunting: A Proactive Approach

In contrast to traditional security measures, threat hunting represents a proactive and iterative approach to identifying and mitigating threats before they can inflict damage. Here are the key characteristics that differentiate threat hunting from traditional security:

Proactive Stance: Threat hunting actively seeks out threats within the environment, focusing on detecting indicators of compromise (IoCs) and suspicious behaviors that may have bypassed traditional security controls. Rather than waiting for alerts from security tools, threat hunters initiate investigations based on hypotheses, threat intelligence, and behavioral patterns. This proactive stance enables organizations to uncover threats that have already infiltrated their systems.

Hypothesis-Driven Methodology: At the core of threat hunting is the hypothesis-driven methodology, where hunters formulate testable hypotheses based on known tactics, techniques, and procedures (TTPs) used by adversaries. This approach allows hunters to investigate specific areas of concern within the environment, focusing their efforts on high-risk targets. In contrast, traditional security measures rely heavily on automated alerts without the context of a well-defined hypothesis.

Iterative Process: Threat hunting is an iterative process that involves continuous monitoring, investigation, and refinement of tactics. Hunters learn from each engagement, adapting their strategies based on emerging threats and lessons learned from past incidents. This iterative approach fosters a culture of continuous improvement and agility in response to evolving threats.

Enhanced Visibility and Context: Threat hunting emphasizes comprehensive data collection and analysis, providing greater visibility into network activities and user behaviors. Hunters leverage a wide array of data sources, including logs, network traffic, and endpoint telemetry, to develop a holistic understanding of their environment. This enhanced visibility allows for the identification of anomalies and potential threats that may be overlooked by traditional security measures.

Integration of Threat Intelligence: Threat hunting heavily relies on threat intelligence to inform investigations and guide hunting efforts. By integrating external threat intelligence with internal data, threat hunters gain insights into the tactics used by adversaries, enabling them to anticipate and mitigate potential attacks. This contrasts with traditional security measures, which may not fully utilize threat intelligence to inform security decisions.

Focus on Adversary Behavior: Threat hunting places a strong emphasis on understanding adversary behavior and motivations. By analyzing the actions of threat actors, hunters can identify patterns that indicate potential compromises. This behavioral focus allows organizations to adapt their defenses to counter emerging threats, rather than merely responding to alerts triggered by known indicators.

Collaboration and Communication: Threat hunting encourages collaboration between different teams within an organization, including security operations, incident response, and threat intelligence teams. This collaboration fosters a shared understanding of threats and enables more effective responses. In contrast, traditional security often operates in silos, limiting information sharing and hindering overall effectiveness.

The Complementary Nature of Threat Hunting and Traditional Security

While threat hunting and traditional security measures are distinct, they are not mutually exclusive. In fact, they complement each other in building a robust cybersecurity posture. Traditional security measures lay the groundwork for a secure environment by establishing preventive controls, while threat hunting enhances the ability to detect and respond to threats that may have bypassed those defenses.

Organizations should aim to integrate threat hunting into their overall security strategy, leveraging the strengths of both approaches. By combining proactive threat hunting with traditional security measures, organizations can create a layered defense that is better equipped to anticipate and mitigate evolving cyber threats.

In conclusion, differentiating threat hunting from traditional security measures is essential for organizations striving to improve their cybersecurity posture. Traditional security approaches emphasize preventive controls and reactive responses, often leaving organizations vulnerable to advanced threats. In contrast, threat hunting adopts a proactive stance, focusing on identifying and mitigating threats before they escalate. By understanding the distinct characteristics of threat hunting and traditional security, organizations can better allocate resources, enhance their defenses, and cultivate a culture of continuous improvement in their cybersecurity efforts. As the threat landscape continues to evolve, the integration of threat hunting into existing security frameworks will be crucial for organizations seeking to stay ahead of cyber adversaries.

1.3 Key Roles and Responsibilities in Threat Hunting

As organizations increasingly recognize the necessity of proactive threat hunting to enhance their cybersecurity posture, the establishment of clearly defined roles and responsibilities becomes essential. Effective threat hunting requires a collaborative effort from various professionals with diverse skill sets and expertise. This chapter explores the key roles involved in threat hunting, outlining their responsibilities and how they contribute to a cohesive and successful threat hunting program.

1. Threat Hunter

The primary role in threat hunting is that of the Threat Hunter, whose main responsibility is to proactively search for indicators of compromise (IoCs) and malicious activities within an organization's network and systems. Key responsibilities include:

- **Conducting Investigations**: Threat hunters analyze data from various sources, including logs, network traffic, and endpoint telemetry, to identify potential threats and anomalies.
- **Formulating Hypotheses**: Based on threat intelligence and previous incidents, threat hunters develop testable hypotheses to guide their investigations and focus on high-risk areas.
- **Leveraging Tools and Technologies**: Proficient in using threat hunting tools, such as SIEM (Security Information and Event Management) systems, EDR (Endpoint Detection and Response) solutions, and behavioral analytics platforms, threat hunters extract and analyze data effectively.
- **Collaborating with Teams**: Threat hunters work closely with incident response teams, threat intelligence analysts, and security operations teams to share findings and insights, fostering a collaborative security environment.
- **Documenting Findings**: Maintaining detailed records of investigations, methodologies, and outcomes is essential for tracking the effectiveness of threat hunting efforts and refining future strategies.

2. Incident Responder

The Incident Responder plays a crucial role in the broader context of threat hunting by focusing on the response to security incidents and breaches. While their primary function is reactive, they must work in conjunction with threat hunters to ensure an effective incident management process. Key responsibilities include:

- **Analyzing Security Incidents**: Incident responders investigate security alerts and determine the nature and scope of incidents, using insights gained from threat hunters to inform their assessments.
- **Coordinating Response Efforts**: They are responsible for coordinating the organization's response to incidents, including containment, eradication, and recovery processes.
- **Implementing Remediation Measures**: After identifying the root cause of an incident, incident responders implement measures to remediate vulnerabilities and prevent future occurrences.
- **Conducting Post-Incident Analysis**: Incident responders analyze the effectiveness of the response and document lessons learned, providing valuable feedback to threat hunters for refining detection strategies.

3. Threat Intelligence Analyst

The Threat Intelligence Analyst plays a critical role in providing the context and insights needed for effective threat hunting. They gather, analyze, and disseminate threat intelligence to support proactive defense strategies. Key responsibilities include:

- **Collecting Threat Intelligence**: Threat intelligence analysts gather information from a variety of sources, including open-source intelligence (OSINT), dark web monitoring, and threat intelligence feeds.
- **Analyzing Adversary Tactics**: They study the tactics, techniques, and procedures (TTPs) employed by threat actors, providing valuable insights that inform threat hunting hypotheses.
- **Disseminating Intelligence**: Sharing relevant threat intelligence with threat hunters and incident responders is crucial for enhancing situational awareness and guiding investigations.
- **Monitoring Emerging Threats**: Threat intelligence analysts stay informed about new threats and vulnerabilities, ensuring that the organization's threat hunting efforts are aligned with the evolving threat landscape.

4. Security Operations Center (SOC) Analyst

The SOC Analyst is an integral part of an organization's cybersecurity team, responsible for monitoring and responding to security events. While their primary focus is on operational security, they play a supporting role in threat hunting efforts. Key responsibilities include:

- **Monitoring Security Alerts**: SOC analysts continuously monitor security alerts generated by security tools, such as SIEMs and IDS, and escalate potential threats to threat hunters for further investigation.
- **Initial Triage**: They perform initial triage of security alerts, categorizing incidents based on severity and determining whether they require deeper investigation by threat hunters.
- **Documenting Security Events**: SOC analysts maintain detailed logs and documentation of security events, providing a historical context that can inform threat hunting activities.
- **Collaboration**: SOC analysts work closely with threat hunters to share insights and findings, facilitating a unified approach to threat detection and response.

5. Forensic Analyst

The Forensic Analyst specializes in investigating security incidents, focusing on collecting, preserving, and analyzing digital evidence to understand the nature of an attack. While not always directly involved in threat hunting, they provide essential support in post-incident investigations. Key responsibilities include:

- **Collecting Digital Evidence**: Forensic analysts collect and preserve digital evidence from compromised systems to ensure that it remains intact for analysis and legal purposes.
- **Analyzing Malicious Activity**: They examine artifacts left by attackers, such as malware, log files, and network traffic, to uncover the techniques and methods used in the attack.
- **Providing Insights**: Forensic analysts share their findings with threat hunters and incident responders, contributing to a better understanding of attacker behavior and informing future threat hunting efforts.

6. Security Architect

The Security Architect plays a strategic role in designing and implementing an organization's cybersecurity infrastructure, ensuring that it is capable of supporting proactive threat hunting initiatives. Key responsibilities include:

- **Designing Security Frameworks**: Security architects develop security frameworks and policies that enable effective threat hunting, including data collection, monitoring, and analysis processes.
- **Implementing Security Controls**: They work to integrate security controls and technologies that support threat detection and hunting, ensuring that the organization has the necessary tools in place.
- **Assessing Security Posture**: Security architects regularly assess the organization's security posture and recommend improvements to enhance the effectiveness of threat hunting efforts.

7. Management and Leadership

Effective threat hunting requires support from management and leadership, who play a crucial role in fostering a culture of cybersecurity within the organization. Key responsibilities include:

- **Setting Strategic Direction**: Management sets the overall strategy and objectives for threat hunting initiatives, aligning them with the organization's broader cybersecurity goals.

- **Allocating Resources**: Leadership is responsible for allocating the necessary resources, including personnel, tools, and training, to support a successful threat hunting program.
- **Promoting a Security Culture**: Management fosters a culture of security awareness and collaboration across departments, emphasizing the importance of proactive threat detection and response.

In conclusion, effective threat hunting relies on a collaborative effort among various roles, each contributing unique expertise and responsibilities. By clearly defining these roles and fostering a culture of teamwork and communication, organizations can enhance their ability to proactively identify and mitigate threats. As the threat landscape continues to evolve, the importance of a well-structured threat hunting team becomes increasingly critical in safeguarding organizational assets and ensuring a robust cybersecurity posture. By understanding the key roles and responsibilities involved in threat hunting, organizations can build a resilient defense against the ever-growing array of cyber threats.

Chapter 2: Understanding the Cyber Kill Chain

In this chapter, we will dissect the cyber kill chain model, a vital framework for understanding the stages of a cyber attack. The kill chain illustrates the various phases an attacker goes through, from initial reconnaissance to the ultimate goal of data exfiltration or system compromise. By breaking down each phase, we can gain valuable insights into the tactics, techniques, and procedures (TTPs) employed by threat actors. Understanding the cyber kill chain is crucial for threat hunters, as it enables them to identify and disrupt attacks at different stages, effectively neutralizing threats before they can achieve their objectives. Additionally, we will examine real-world examples to demonstrate how organizations have successfully utilized the kill chain model to enhance their security posture. Through this exploration, you will develop a comprehensive understanding of how to apply the cyber kill chain to inform your threat hunting strategies and improve your organization's defense mechanisms.

2.1 Detailed Breakdown of Each Kill Chain Phase

The Cyber Kill Chain, developed by Lockheed Martin, is a structured framework that outlines the various stages of a cyber attack. Understanding each phase of the Kill Chain is crucial for organizations seeking to bolster their defenses through effective threat hunting and incident response. This chapter will provide a detailed breakdown of each phase, highlighting the key activities performed by attackers and the corresponding defensive measures that organizations can implement to disrupt or mitigate these attacks.

1. Reconnaissance

Overview: The reconnaissance phase is the initial stage of the Kill Chain, where attackers gather information about their target to identify vulnerabilities and potential entry points. This phase is critical because the information gathered will inform the attack strategy.

Activities:

- **Information Gathering**: Attackers may use open-source intelligence (OSINT) tools to collect data from various sources, including social media, company websites, domain registrations, and public records.

- **Network Scanning**: Attackers often use network scanning tools (e.g., Nmap) to map the organization's network, identifying active IP addresses, open ports, and services running on those ports.
- **Identifying Employees**: Social engineering techniques may be employed to identify key personnel within the organization, making it easier to craft targeted phishing attacks later.

Defensive Measures:

- **Threat Intelligence**: Organizations can utilize threat intelligence to stay informed about the tactics, techniques, and procedures (TTPs) commonly used by attackers in the reconnaissance phase.
- **Security Awareness Training**: Conducting regular training sessions for employees can help them recognize social engineering attempts and reduce the risk of information leaks.
- **Network Segmentation**: Properly segmenting networks can limit the information available to attackers and reduce their ability to conduct effective reconnaissance.

2. Weaponization

Overview: In the weaponization phase, attackers create a malicious payload tailored to exploit the vulnerabilities identified during reconnaissance. This phase often involves combining an exploit with a backdoor into a deliverable payload.

Activities:

- **Creating Malware**: Attackers may develop or modify malware (e.g., ransomware, trojans) that exploits specific vulnerabilities discovered during the reconnaissance phase.
- **Phishing Preparation**: Attackers package the malware into a deliverable format, such as a malicious email attachment or a link to a compromised website, designed to trick victims into executing the payload.

Defensive Measures:

- **Email Filtering**: Implementing advanced email filtering solutions can help detect and block phishing emails containing malicious attachments or links.
- **File Integrity Monitoring**: Monitoring files for unauthorized changes can help detect the presence of malware or other unauthorized changes to systems.

- **Endpoint Protection**: Utilizing endpoint protection solutions that can detect and block malicious payloads before they are executed is crucial for defense.

3. Delivery

Overview: The delivery phase is when the attacker transmits the weaponized payload to the target. This can occur through various means, such as email, removable media, or direct network connections.

Activities:

- **Phishing Emails**: Attackers often deliver malware through phishing emails that appear legitimate to encourage recipients to open attachments or click on malicious links.
- **Exploiting Vulnerabilities**: Attackers may also leverage network vulnerabilities to deliver malware directly to exposed systems.

Defensive Measures:

- **User Training**: Educating employees on how to recognize phishing emails and other social engineering tactics can significantly reduce the risk of successful delivery.
- **Sandboxing**: Implementing sandboxing techniques allows suspicious emails and attachments to be executed in a controlled environment for analysis before reaching the end user.
- **Network Intrusion Prevention Systems (NIPS)**: Deploying NIPS can help detect and block malicious network traffic, preventing unauthorized delivery of payloads.

4. Exploitation

Overview: In the exploitation phase, the attacker executes the malicious payload to gain access to the target system. This is a critical moment in the attack, as it marks the transition from delivery to compromise.

Activities:

- **Executing the Payload**: The attacker's malware executes, exploiting the vulnerability to gain unauthorized access to the system.

- **Privilege Escalation**: Once the attacker has access, they may attempt to escalate their privileges to gain higher levels of access within the network.

Defensive Measures:

- **Patch Management**: Regularly updating and patching systems and applications helps mitigate known vulnerabilities that attackers may exploit.
- **Application Whitelisting**: Implementing application whitelisting can prevent unauthorized applications from executing on systems, reducing the risk of exploitation.
- **Behavioral Analysis**: Employing behavioral analysis tools can help identify unusual activities that may indicate exploitation, allowing for early intervention.

5. Installation

Overview: After successfully exploiting a system, the attacker aims to establish a foothold by installing additional malware or backdoors. This phase ensures the attacker retains access to the compromised system even if initial access methods are detected and removed.

Activities:

- **Installing Backdoors**: Attackers often install persistent backdoors that allow them to re-enter the system at will.
- **Command and Control (C2)**: The malware may establish communication with a remote server, allowing the attacker to issue commands and control the compromised system.

Defensive Measures:

- **Endpoint Detection and Response (EDR)**: EDR solutions can monitor endpoint activities and detect the presence of malicious installations or unauthorized software.
- **Network Segmentation**: Segmenting critical systems can limit the impact of a successful installation, restricting the attacker's lateral movement within the network.
- **Regular Audits**: Conducting regular security audits and assessments can help identify unauthorized installations or backdoors on systems.

6. Command and Control (C2)

Overview: Once a backdoor is installed, the attacker establishes a command and control (C2) channel, enabling them to remotely control the compromised system and execute additional malicious activities.

Activities:

- **Establishing Communication**: The malware communicates with the attacker's C2 server to receive instructions and send back data.
- **Data Exfiltration**: Attackers may use the C2 channel to exfiltrate sensitive data from the compromised system.

Defensive Measures:

- **Monitoring Network Traffic**: Continuous monitoring of outbound network traffic can help identify unusual communication patterns indicative of C2 activity.
- **DNS Filtering**: Implementing DNS filtering can block access to known malicious domains associated with C2 servers.
- **Threat Intelligence Integration**: Integrating threat intelligence feeds can provide visibility into known C2 infrastructures, enhancing detection capabilities.

7. Actions on Objectives

Overview: In the final phase of the Kill Chain, the attacker achieves their primary objectives, which may include data theft, system manipulation, or disruption of services. This phase is often characterized by the realization of the attacker's goals.

Activities:

- **Data Theft**: Attackers may steal sensitive data, such as personally identifiable information (PII), intellectual property, or financial information.
- **Lateral Movement**: Attackers may attempt to move laterally within the network to compromise additional systems and gather more information.
- **Disruption**: In some cases, the objective may be to disrupt business operations, such as deploying ransomware to encrypt critical data.

Defensive Measures:

- **Data Loss Prevention (DLP):** Implementing DLP solutions can help monitor and prevent unauthorized data exfiltration from the organization.

- **Incident Response Planning**: Developing and regularly testing incident response plans ensures that organizations are prepared to respond effectively when a breach occurs.
- **Regular Security Audits**: Conducting security audits and vulnerability assessments can help organizations identify weaknesses and improve their overall security posture.

Understanding the detailed phases of the Cyber Kill Chain is essential for organizations looking to enhance their threat hunting and incident response capabilities. By recognizing the key activities performed by attackers at each phase, organizations can implement targeted defensive measures to disrupt attacks before they reach their objectives. The Kill Chain framework not only provides a roadmap for attackers but also serves as a guide for defenders to proactively identify and mitigate potential threats. By integrating Kill Chain insights into their cybersecurity strategies, organizations can strengthen their defenses and better protect their critical assets from evolving cyber threats.

2.2 The Role of Threat Actors in the Kill Chain

Understanding the role of threat actors in the Cyber Kill Chain is crucial for organizations aiming to fortify their cybersecurity defenses. Threat actors, also known as adversaries or attackers, are individuals or groups that engage in malicious activities to exploit vulnerabilities for financial gain, political motives, or other malicious purposes. This chapter examines the various types of threat actors, their motivations, and how they operate within the phases of the Kill Chain. By recognizing their roles, organizations can tailor their defenses and threat-hunting strategies more effectively.

1. Types of Threat Actors

Threat actors can be categorized based on their motivations, skills, and resources. The following are the primary types of threat actors that organizations may encounter:

a. Cybercriminals

- **Motivation**: Primarily financial gain.
- **Profile**: Often organized groups or individuals who exploit vulnerabilities to steal data, deploy ransomware, or engage in fraud.
- **Kill Chain Role**: Cybercriminals typically engage in all phases of the Kill Chain, from reconnaissance to actions on objectives. They may conduct extensive

research to identify targets, deploy malware, and exfiltrate sensitive information for monetary gain.

b. Nation-State Actors

- **Motivation**: Political, economic, or strategic advantages.
- **Profile**: Government-sponsored hackers or intelligence agencies who seek to gain insights into foreign governments, steal sensitive data, or disrupt critical infrastructure.
- **Kill Chain Role**: Nation-state actors often engage in sophisticated and prolonged campaigns, focusing heavily on reconnaissance and persistence. They are skilled in social engineering tactics and often employ advanced malware that is difficult to detect.

c. Hacktivists

- **Motivation**: Political or social causes.
- **Profile**: Individuals or groups who use hacking to promote their ideological beliefs or agendas. They may target organizations that they perceive as unethical or corrupt.
- **Kill Chain Role**: Hacktivists may engage in reconnaissance to identify high-profile targets, often leveraging publicly available information. Their actions typically culminate in data leaks, website defacements, or distributed denial-of-service (DDoS) attacks, focusing on creating public awareness of their causes.

d. Insider Threats

- **Motivation**: Personal grievances, financial gain, or coercion.
- **Profile**: Employees, contractors, or partners with legitimate access to organizational resources who exploit their privileges for malicious purposes.
- **Kill Chain Role**: Insider threats may skip the initial reconnaissance phase since they already have intimate knowledge of the organization's systems. They can directly engage in exploitation, installation of backdoors, and actions on objectives, posing unique challenges due to their legitimate access.

e. Script Kiddies

- **Motivation**: Reputation, thrill-seeking, or mischief.
- **Profile**: Less skilled individuals who use pre-built scripts or tools to exploit known vulnerabilities without a deep understanding of how they work.

- **Kill Chain Role**: Script kiddies typically focus on simpler exploits, relying on publicly available tools. Their attacks may be less sophisticated but can still cause significant disruption if they successfully exploit vulnerabilities.

2. Threat Actor Motivations

Understanding the motivations behind different types of threat actors is essential for effective threat hunting and defense strategies. Here are some common motivations that drive threat actors:

a. Financial Gain

Cybercriminals are primarily motivated by the potential for profit. Their attacks often involve stealing credit card information, deploying ransomware, or engaging in various forms of fraud. Financial gain is a powerful motivator that can drive sophisticated and persistent attacks.

b. Political and Ideological Objectives

Nation-state actors and hacktivists often engage in cyber activities to promote political agendas or achieve strategic goals. Their attacks may focus on espionage, data theft, or disruption of critical infrastructure to further their objectives.

c. Revenge or Grievance

Insider threats may stem from personal grievances, such as feeling undervalued or mistreated within an organization. These individuals may exploit their access to settle scores or retaliate against their employer.

d. Reputation and Recognition

Script kiddies or less skilled hackers may be motivated by the desire for recognition among their peers. By successfully launching attacks or gaining notoriety in the hacking community, they seek to build their reputations, even if their actions are less consequential.

3. Threat Actor Tactics, Techniques, and Procedures (TTPs)

Threat actors utilize specific tactics, techniques, and procedures (TTPs) that can vary based on their motivations and capabilities. Understanding these TTPs is critical for organizations to detect and respond to threats effectively. Here are some common TTPs employed by threat actors throughout the Kill Chain:

a. Reconnaissance Tactics

- **Open-Source Intelligence (OSINT):** Attackers often utilize publicly available information to gather insights into potential targets, employees, and vulnerabilities.
- **Social Engineering**: Threat actors may engage in social engineering to manipulate individuals into revealing sensitive information or granting access to systems.

b. Delivery Techniques

- **Phishing Campaigns**: Cybercriminals frequently use phishing emails to deliver malicious payloads, tricking users into clicking on links or downloading attachments.
- **Exploitation of Vulnerabilities**: Attackers may leverage known software vulnerabilities to gain unauthorized access or deliver malware.

c. Exploitation Methods

- **Malware Deployment**: Attackers often use various types of malware, such as ransomware, keyloggers, or remote access Trojans (RATs), to exploit vulnerabilities and gain a foothold.
- **Credential Theft**: Techniques such as credential dumping or keylogging can be used to harvest user credentials, enabling further access to systems.

d. Command and Control (C2) Techniques

- **Establishing C2 Channels**: Attackers create communication channels with compromised systems, often utilizing techniques such as domain generation algorithms (DGAs) or encrypted traffic to evade detection.
- **Data Exfiltration Methods**: Threat actors may employ steganography or other obfuscation techniques to exfiltrate sensitive data from the target environment.

e. Actions on Objectives

- **Data Theft**: Many threat actors aim to steal sensitive data for financial gain, espionage, or political purposes.

- **Disruption and Sabotage**: Some actors may seek to disrupt operations or damage an organization's reputation through denial-of-service attacks or data destruction.

4. Implications for Threat Hunting

Understanding the role of threat actors in the Kill Chain has significant implications for organizations seeking to implement effective threat hunting programs. Here are several key considerations:

a. Tailored Threat Hunting Strategies

Organizations must tailor their threat hunting strategies based on the types of threat actors they are likely to encounter. For instance, a financial institution may prioritize defenses against cybercriminals and insider threats, while a government agency may focus on nation-state actors.

b. Integration of Threat Intelligence

Utilizing threat intelligence that provides insights into the TTPs of known threat actors can enhance an organization's ability to detect and respond to threats. By staying informed about emerging threats and attacker motivations, organizations can adapt their hunting strategies accordingly.

c. Employee Training and Awareness

Given that social engineering and insider threats are common attack vectors, organizations should invest in employee training and awareness programs to help staff recognize and report suspicious activities. This proactive approach can strengthen defenses against various threat actors.

d. Continuous Monitoring and Adaptation

As threat actors evolve their tactics, organizations must continuously monitor their environments and adapt their defenses accordingly. Regular assessments of the effectiveness of threat hunting efforts can help identify gaps and inform future strategies.

In conclusion, understanding the role of threat actors in the Cyber Kill Chain is essential for organizations seeking to enhance their cybersecurity defenses. By categorizing threat actors based on their motivations and tactics, organizations can develop targeted strategies for detecting and mitigating threats. The knowledge of TTPs employed by various actors further empowers organizations to strengthen their threat hunting efforts and improve their overall security posture. As the threat landscape continues to evolve, a deep understanding of threat actors will be key to effectively anticipating, detecting, and responding to cyber threats.

2.3 How to Disrupt the Kill Chain Effectively

Disrupting the Cyber Kill Chain is crucial for organizations aiming to enhance their cybersecurity posture and thwart potential attacks before they can achieve their objectives. By understanding the various phases of the Kill Chain and employing targeted strategies, organizations can significantly reduce their vulnerability to cyber threats. This chapter outlines practical approaches to effectively disrupt the Kill Chain at each phase, empowering organizations to defend against a wide range of adversaries.

1. Reconnaissance Disruption

The reconnaissance phase is where attackers gather intelligence about their targets. Disrupting this phase involves making it difficult for threat actors to collect useful information.

a. Limit Public Exposure

- **Secure Sensitive Information**: Ensure that sensitive information, such as employee directories and infrastructure details, is not publicly accessible. Regularly audit your organization's web presence to identify and remove any unnecessary public data.
- **Use Privacy Settings**: Encourage employees to use privacy settings on social media platforms to limit the visibility of their profiles and personal information.

b. Implement Active Defense Techniques

- **Honeypots**: Deploy honeypots or decoy systems to lure attackers into interacting with a controlled environment. This can provide valuable insights into the methods and tools used by attackers while distracting them from real assets.
- **Threat Intelligence Sharing**: Participate in information-sharing initiatives with industry peers to stay informed about emerging threats and tactics used in reconnaissance.

c. Conduct Security Awareness Training

- **Educate Employees**: Regularly train employees on recognizing social engineering tactics, phishing attempts, and suspicious behavior. An informed workforce is less likely to fall victim to reconnaissance efforts by attackers.

2. Weaponization Disruption

In the weaponization phase, attackers create malicious payloads. Organizations can disrupt this phase by making it challenging for attackers to develop effective exploits.

a. Patch Management

- **Regular Updates**: Implement a robust patch management program to ensure that all software and systems are updated with the latest security patches. This reduces the number of vulnerabilities that attackers can exploit.
- **Vulnerability Scanning**: Regularly conduct vulnerability assessments to identify and remediate weaknesses before they can be weaponized by attackers.

b. Secure Software Development Lifecycle (SDLC)

- **Code Reviews and Testing**: Integrate security measures into the software development process, including regular code reviews and security testing. By identifying vulnerabilities early, organizations can reduce the likelihood of them being weaponized.
- **Threat Modeling**: Engage in threat modeling during the design phase of applications to anticipate potential attack vectors and mitigate risks proactively.

c. Monitor for Malicious Activity

- **Anomaly Detection**: Implement anomaly detection systems to identify unusual patterns that may indicate the development or testing of malicious payloads within the network.

3. Delivery Disruption

Disrupting the delivery phase involves preventing attackers from successfully transmitting their malicious payloads to their targets.

a. Advanced Email Filtering

- **Email Security Solutions**: Utilize advanced email security solutions that employ machine learning algorithms to identify and block phishing emails and malicious attachments before they reach users' inboxes.
- **Domain-Based Message** Authentication: Implement authentication protocols such as DMARC, DKIM, and SPF to validate the legitimacy of incoming emails and prevent email spoofing.

b. Network Segmentation

- **Isolate Critical Systems**: Segment the network to limit access to sensitive systems and data. This can reduce the attack surface and make it more difficult for attackers to deliver their payloads effectively.
- **Controlled Access**: Implement strict access controls and least privilege principles to ensure that only authorized users can access critical resources.

c. User Education and Awareness

- **Phishing Simulations**: Conduct simulated phishing campaigns to test employee awareness and resilience. This can help identify vulnerabilities in the organization's human defenses and improve response protocols.

4. Exploitation Disruption

The exploitation phase is when attackers execute their payloads to compromise systems. Effective disruption strategies can minimize the risk of successful exploitation.

a. Endpoint Protection

- **Advanced Endpoint Security Solutions**: Deploy endpoint protection solutions that utilize behavior-based detection techniques to identify and block suspicious activities in real time.
- **Application Whitelisting**: Implement application whitelisting to prevent unauthorized applications from executing on endpoints. This can mitigate the risk of malicious payloads being executed.

b. Continuous Monitoring

- **Real-Time Monitoring**: Establish continuous monitoring of network and system activities to identify signs of exploitation attempts. Implement Security Information and Event Management (SIEM) solutions to aggregate and analyze logs for anomalies.
- **Threat Hunting**: Conduct regular threat hunting exercises to proactively search for indicators of compromise (IoCs) and suspicious activities that may indicate exploitation attempts.

c. Security Configuration Management

- **Hardening Systems**: Regularly review and harden system configurations to remove unnecessary services, ports, and permissions that could be exploited by attackers.
- **System Audits**: Conduct routine security audits to identify misconfigurations and vulnerabilities that could be targeted during the exploitation phase.

5. Installation Disruption

To prevent attackers from establishing a foothold in the network, organizations can implement strategies to detect and remove malware before it can install itself.

a. Network Traffic Analysis

- **Monitor for C2 Communications**: Implement solutions that analyze network traffic for patterns associated with command and control (C2) communications. Blocking such traffic can hinder an attacker's ability to maintain control over compromised systems.
- **DNS Monitoring**: Monitor DNS queries for unusual or suspicious activity that may indicate the presence of malware attempting to communicate with a C2 server.

b. Endpoint Detection and Response (EDR)

- **Behavioral Analysis**: Utilize EDR solutions that leverage behavioral analysis to detect signs of malware installation and respond promptly to mitigate threats.
- **Automated Response Mechanisms**: Implement automated response capabilities that can isolate compromised systems from the network, preventing further spread of malware.

c. Regular Malware Scans

- **Scheduled Scanning**: Conduct regular malware scans on endpoints to identify and remove any malicious software that may have bypassed initial defenses.
- **Threat Intelligence Integration**: Use threat intelligence feeds to stay updated on emerging malware signatures and techniques, enhancing the detection and removal of known threats.

6. Command and Control (C2) Disruption

Disrupting the command and control phase involves preventing attackers from maintaining remote access to compromised systems.

a. C2 Disruption Strategies

- **Threat Intelligence Monitoring**: Utilize threat intelligence to monitor known C2 infrastructures and block communications to malicious domains or IP addresses.
- **Network Segmentation**: Segment critical systems from external networks to limit the ability of attackers to establish C2 channels.

b. DNS Filtering and Security

- **DNS Filtering Solutions**: Implement DNS filtering solutions that block access to known malicious domains, effectively cutting off attackers from their C2 servers.
- **Regular DNS Audits**: Conduct regular audits of DNS records to identify unauthorized changes or suspicious entries.

c. Incident Response Planning

- **Preparedness Exercises**: Regularly conduct incident response drills focused on C2 disruptions to ensure that the response team is prepared to act quickly if a breach occurs.
- **Incident Response Team**: Establish a dedicated incident response team trained to identify and mitigate C2 communications effectively.

7. Actions on Objectives Disruption

The final phase of the Kill Chain involves the attacker achieving their objectives, such as data theft or service disruption. Disrupting this phase requires a comprehensive strategy to protect critical assets.

a. Data Loss Prevention (DLP)

- **DLP Solutions**: Implement DLP solutions that monitor and restrict the movement of sensitive data outside the organization. These solutions can help prevent data exfiltration during an attack.
- **Policy Enforcement**: Develop and enforce policies that dictate how sensitive data can be accessed, shared, and transmitted.

b. Continuous Monitoring and Auditing

- **Real-Time Alerts**: Set up real-time alerting mechanisms for suspicious activities related to data access and transfer, enabling a swift response to potential data breaches.
- **Access Logs Review**: Regularly review access logs to identify unusual access patterns that may indicate unauthorized actions taken by an attacker.

c. Incident Response and Recovery

- **Incident Response Plans**: Develop comprehensive incident response plans that outline the steps to take in the event of a successful breach. Ensure that these plans are regularly tested and updated.
- **Backup and Recovery**: Maintain regular backups of critical data and systems to ensure rapid recovery in the event of data loss or ransomware attacks.

Effectively disrupting the Cyber Kill Chain requires a multi-layered approach that encompasses technical, procedural, and human elements. By implementing targeted strategies to address each phase of the Kill Chain, organizations can significantly reduce their risk of successful attacks and enhance their overall security posture. The proactive measures outlined in this chapter not only help organizations prevent breaches but also empower them to respond quickly and effectively when incidents occur. As the threat landscape continues to evolve, staying vigilant and adaptable will be key to successfully disrupting the Kill Chain and safeguarding critical assets.

Chapter 3: The Threat Landscape Today

In this chapter, we will explore the current threat landscape, where cyber attacks are not only more frequent but also increasingly sophisticated. We will analyze the diverse array of adversaries, from lone hackers to organized crime syndicates and nation-state actors, each employing unique tactics to exploit vulnerabilities. By examining recent high-profile cyber incidents, we will highlight the impact of threats such as ransomware, phishing, and advanced persistent threats (APTs) on organizations across various sectors. This chapter will also delve into emerging trends and technologies shaping the threat landscape, emphasizing the importance of staying informed about the evolving tactics and motivations of cybercriminals. By understanding the intricacies of today's threats, you will be better equipped to anticipate potential attacks and implement effective threat hunting strategies tailored to the unique challenges your organization faces. This foundational knowledge will pave the way for more advanced discussions in the subsequent chapters as we delve deeper into proactive defense mechanisms.

3.1 Analyzing Recent High-Profile Cyber Attacks

In the rapidly evolving landscape of cybersecurity, high-profile cyber attacks serve as critical case studies that highlight both the vulnerabilities of organizations and the sophistication of modern threat actors. Analyzing these attacks provides valuable insights into the tactics, techniques, and procedures (TTPs) employed by adversaries, as well as the potential impact on targeted organizations. This chapter focuses on several recent high-profile cyber attacks, examining their characteristics, methodologies, and the lessons learned to enhance future defenses.

1. Overview of High-Profile Cyber Attacks

High-profile cyber attacks typically involve significant data breaches, ransomware incidents, or disruptions to critical services. They often attract widespread media attention due to their scale, impact, and the entities involved. Analyzing such attacks can reveal common patterns in attacker behavior and the security weaknesses that enabled the breaches.

2. Case Studies

a. SolarWinds Supply Chain Attack (2020)

Overview: The SolarWinds attack involved a sophisticated supply chain compromise where threat actors injected malicious code into the company's Orion software platform, impacting thousands of organizations, including U.S. government agencies and Fortune 500 companies.

Attack Methodology:

- **Reconnaissance**: The attackers conducted extensive reconnaissance to identify vulnerabilities in SolarWinds' development environment.
- **Weaponization**: Malicious code, known as "SUNBURST," was embedded into software updates.
- **Delivery and Exploitation**: The compromised updates were distributed to SolarWinds customers, enabling attackers to gain unauthorized access to networks.
- **C2 Communication**: Attackers established covert command and control channels to maintain persistent access.
- **Impact**: The breach exposed sensitive data and highlighted vulnerabilities in supply chain security across various industries. It also raised concerns about national security given the involvement of government agencies.

Lessons Learned:

- **Supply Chain Security**: Organizations must implement rigorous supply chain security measures, including monitoring and auditing third-party software updates.
- **Detection and Response**: The need for improved detection capabilities, including anomaly detection and threat hunting, was underscored by the delayed discovery of the attack.

b. Colonial Pipeline Ransomware Attack (2021)

Overview: In May 2021, Colonial Pipeline, a major U.S. fuel pipeline operator, fell victim to a ransomware attack that disrupted fuel supply across the eastern United States.

Attack Methodology:

- **Initial Access**: Attackers gained access to Colonial Pipeline's network through compromised credentials obtained from a third-party vendor.
- **Deployment of Ransomware**: The ransomware, known as DarkSide, encrypted the company's data and demanded a ransom for decryption.

- **C2 and Data Exfiltration**: Attackers communicated with their C2 servers and exfiltrated sensitive data prior to encryption.
- **Impact**: The attack led to fuel shortages, panic buying, and significant economic disruption. Colonial Pipeline ultimately paid a ransom of approximately $4.4 million.

Lessons Learned:

- **Credential Management**: Organizations should implement strong credential management practices, including multi-factor authentication (MFA) and regular password changes.
- **Incident Response Preparedness**: The attack highlighted the need for robust incident response plans and the importance of conducting regular drills to prepare for ransomware scenarios.

c. Microsoft Exchange Server Vulnerabilities (2021)

Overview: In early 2021, Microsoft disclosed critical vulnerabilities in its Exchange Server software, which were actively exploited by threat actors to gain access to email accounts and sensitive data.

Attack Methodology:

- **Exploitation of Zero-Day Vulnerabilities**: Attackers exploited four zero-day vulnerabilities to bypass authentication and gain remote access to Exchange Servers.
- **Web Shell Deployment**: After gaining access, attackers deployed web shells to maintain persistence and control over compromised servers.
- **Data Theft and Lateral Movement**: Attackers moved laterally within networks, stealing sensitive information and installing additional malware.
- **Impact**: The attack affected tens of thousands of organizations globally, leading to significant data breaches and compromising sensitive information.

Lessons Learned:

- **Timely Patch Management**: The attack underscored the importance of timely patch management and vulnerability assessments to mitigate the risk of exploitation.
- **Defense-in-Depth**: Organizations should adopt a defense-in-depth approach, employing multiple layers of security controls to protect critical systems.

d. Kaseya VSA Ransomware Attack (2021)

Overview: The Kaseya VSA attack involved the exploitation of vulnerabilities in Kaseya's remote monitoring and management software, impacting managed service providers (MSPs) and their clients.

Attack Methodology:

- **Supply Chain Attack**: Attackers exploited vulnerabilities in the Kaseya VSA platform to distribute ransomware to numerous MSPs and their customers.
- **Widespread Distribution**: The ransomware, REvil, encrypted data across hundreds of organizations.
- **Impact**: The attack affected around 1,500 organizations globally, disrupting operations and leading to significant financial losses.

Lessons Learned:

- **Third-Party Risk Management**: Organizations must enhance their third-party risk management practices to ensure the security of software vendors and partners.
- **Incident Response Coordination**: Effective coordination with law enforcement and cybersecurity agencies is crucial during large-scale incidents.

3. Common Patterns and Insights

The analysis of these high-profile cyber attacks reveals several common patterns and insights:

Supply Chain Vulnerabilities: Many recent attacks exploit vulnerabilities within the software supply chain, highlighting the importance of securing third-party software and vendor relationships.

Human Element: Social engineering and credential theft remain prevalent tactics among attackers, underscoring the need for comprehensive security training and awareness programs.

Proactive Defense Measures: Organizations that adopt proactive defense measures, including regular vulnerability assessments, timely patch management, and incident response planning, are better equipped to prevent and mitigate attacks.

Importance of Threat Intelligence: Continuous monitoring of threat intelligence can help organizations stay informed about emerging threats and vulnerabilities, allowing them to adapt their defenses accordingly.

The analysis of recent high-profile cyber attacks provides critical insights into the evolving threat landscape and the tactics employed by modern threat actors. By understanding the methodologies and motivations behind these attacks, organizations can enhance their cybersecurity strategies, bolster defenses, and mitigate the risks posed by cyber threats. Continuous learning from past incidents is vital for organizations striving to stay one step ahead in the ongoing battle against cybercrime. As the threat landscape continues to evolve, it is imperative for organizations to remain vigilant, adaptive, and prepared for the challenges that lie ahead.

3.2 The Impact of Ransomware on Organizations

Ransomware has become one of the most pervasive and destructive forms of cybercrime, targeting organizations across various sectors, from healthcare and finance to education and critical infrastructure. As ransomware attacks continue to escalate in frequency and sophistication, understanding their impact on organizations is essential for developing effective response strategies. This chapter explores the multifaceted effects of ransomware attacks on organizations, delving into the immediate and long-term consequences, as well as the broader implications for the cybersecurity landscape.

1. Overview of Ransomware Attacks

Ransomware is a type of malware that encrypts a victim's files, rendering them inaccessible until a ransom is paid to the attacker. These attacks can vary in complexity, from basic encryption to more sophisticated methods involving data exfiltration and double extortion tactics, where attackers threaten to leak sensitive data if the ransom is not paid. The rise of ransomware-as-a-service (RaaS) has further democratized access to ransomware tools, enabling even low-skilled attackers to launch devastating attacks.

2. Immediate Consequences of Ransomware Attacks

The immediate effects of a ransomware attack can be severe and disruptive, impacting organizations in several ways:

a. Operational Disruption

- **Downtime**: Ransomware attacks often lead to significant operational downtime, as organizations scramble to respond to the incident and restore access to encrypted systems. This downtime can vary from hours to weeks, depending on the organization's preparedness and response capabilities.
- **Loss of Productivity**: Employees may be unable to perform their duties during the attack, leading to a loss of productivity that can ripple through the organization. Critical functions, such as customer service and supply chain operations, may be halted, resulting in further operational delays.

b. Financial Impact

- **Ransom Payments**: Organizations faced with ransomware attacks may opt to pay the ransom to regain access to their data, leading to substantial financial losses. The average ransom demand has increased significantly, often reaching hundreds of thousands or even millions of dollars.
- **Recovery Costs**: Even if organizations refuse to pay the ransom, the costs associated with recovery can be staggering. Expenses may include forensic investigations, system restoration, legal fees, and potential regulatory fines. According to cybersecurity firm Coveware, the average cost of recovery from a ransomware attack can exceed $1.85 million.

c. Data Loss and Corruption

- **Loss of Critical Data**: Organizations may suffer permanent data loss if they do not have effective backup solutions in place. In some cases, even backups can be compromised during an attack, leaving organizations without vital information.
- **Data Corruption**: Ransomware can corrupt data, making it unusable even if it can be decrypted. This can lead to further complications in recovery efforts.

3. Long-Term Implications of Ransomware Attacks

The impact of ransomware extends beyond immediate disruptions, creating long-term challenges for organizations:

a. Reputational Damage

- **Loss of Trust**: Ransomware attacks can severely damage an organization's reputation, leading to a loss of trust among customers, partners, and

stakeholders. Clients may be hesitant to engage with a company that has experienced a significant security breach.
- **Brand Devaluation**: The long-term effects on a brand can be significant, particularly if the attack results in data breaches that expose sensitive customer information. This can lead to negative media coverage, customer backlash, and decreased market share.

b. Regulatory and Legal Consequences

- **Compliance Issues**: Organizations may face legal and regulatory consequences following a ransomware attack, especially if they are found to be non-compliant with data protection regulations such as GDPR or HIPAA. Fines and sanctions can exacerbate financial losses and complicate recovery efforts.
- **Litigation Risks**: Companies may face lawsuits from customers or partners affected by the breach, leading to costly legal battles and settlements. This risk is particularly pronounced in sectors that handle sensitive data, such as healthcare and finance.

c. Changes in Business Practices

- **Increased Security Spending**: In the wake of a ransomware attack, organizations often increase their cybersecurity budgets to enhance defenses and prevent future incidents. This may involve investing in new technologies, security training, and hiring additional personnel.
- **Reevaluation of Risk Management Strategies**: Organizations may reevaluate their risk management frameworks, adopting a more proactive approach to cybersecurity. This can include developing incident response plans, conducting regular security assessments, and implementing more robust backup and recovery solutions.

4. Broader Implications for the Cybersecurity Landscape

The rise of ransomware attacks has broader implications for the cybersecurity landscape, influencing trends in threat detection, incident response, and overall security strategies:

a. Evolution of Cybersecurity Solutions

- **Advanced Threat Detection**: Organizations are increasingly investing in advanced threat detection solutions that leverage artificial intelligence and machine learning to identify and respond to ransomware threats in real time.
- **Behavioral Analysis**: Security solutions that analyze user behavior and network traffic patterns are gaining prominence, helping organizations detect anomalies that may indicate a ransomware attack.

b. Industry Collaboration

- **Information Sharing Initiatives**: The prevalence of ransomware has prompted greater collaboration among organizations, government agencies, and cybersecurity firms. Information-sharing initiatives enable organizations to exchange intelligence on emerging threats and vulnerabilities, enhancing collective defenses.
- **Public-Private Partnerships**: Governments and private sector entities are increasingly partnering to develop comprehensive strategies to combat ransomware, including public awareness campaigns, threat intelligence sharing, and coordinated response efforts.

c. Policy and Legislative Changes

- **Regulatory Frameworks**: Governments worldwide are responding to the ransomware threat by developing and enforcing stricter cybersecurity regulations. These regulations often mandate reporting of ransomware incidents, improving transparency and accountability.
- **Cybersecurity Funding**: Increased awareness of ransomware's impact has led to calls for greater investment in cybersecurity initiatives at the national and organizational levels, aimed at building resilience against future attacks.

The impact of ransomware on organizations is profound, with immediate operational disruptions and long-term financial, reputational, and regulatory consequences. As ransomware attacks continue to evolve, organizations must remain vigilant, adopting proactive measures to enhance their cybersecurity posture and mitigate the risks associated with these threats. By learning from past incidents and implementing robust defenses, organizations can better prepare for the challenges posed by ransomware and safeguard their critical assets in an increasingly perilous digital landscape.

3.3 Emerging Threats: What to Watch For

As the cybersecurity landscape continues to evolve, organizations face a growing array of emerging threats that challenge traditional defenses and demand proactive strategies. This chapter explores the latest trends in cyber threats, focusing on the techniques, tactics, and procedures (TTPs) being employed by cybercriminals, and the implications these threats have for organizations. By understanding these emerging threats, organizations can enhance their cybersecurity posture and better prepare for the challenges that lie ahead.

1. Overview of Emerging Threats

Emerging threats in the cyber realm are characterized by their novel approaches, increased sophistication, and ability to exploit existing vulnerabilities in systems and processes. These threats often arise from advancements in technology, changes in the threat landscape, and shifts in attacker motivations. Recognizing and understanding these threats is essential for developing effective strategies to mitigate risks.

2. Key Emerging Threats to Watch For

a. Ransomware Evolution

Double Extortion Tactics: Cybercriminals are increasingly adopting double extortion tactics, where they not only encrypt an organization's data but also exfiltrate sensitive information and threaten to leak it if the ransom is not paid. This adds pressure on organizations to comply with ransom demands, as the reputational damage from data leaks can be severe.

Ransomware-as-a-Service (RaaS): The rise of RaaS has made sophisticated ransomware tools accessible to even low-skilled attackers. This proliferation of ransomware kits lowers the barrier to entry for cybercriminals, leading to an increase in the frequency and diversity of attacks.

Targeting Critical Infrastructure: Ransomware attacks are increasingly targeting critical infrastructure sectors, such as healthcare, energy, and transportation. These attacks can have devastating consequences, as they can disrupt essential services and endanger public safety.

b. Supply Chain Attacks

Complex Attack Vectors: Supply chain attacks involve compromising third-party vendors to gain access to larger targets. This tactic was prominently showcased in the

SolarWinds attack, where attackers infiltrated a software supply chain to target numerous organizations.

Increased Risk of Vulnerabilities: As organizations become more interconnected through partnerships and vendor relationships, the risk of vulnerabilities in the supply chain grows. Attackers can exploit these relationships to infiltrate networks, making supply chain security a critical focus area for organizations.

c. Insider Threats

Malicious and Unintentional Threats: Insider threats can originate from employees, contractors, or business partners who either intentionally cause harm or unintentionally expose the organization to risks through negligence. The motivations for malicious insider threats can range from financial gain to personal grievances.

Heightened Risk During Remote Work: The shift to remote work has exacerbated the risk of insider threats, as employees may have access to sensitive information outside the secure environment of the office. Organizations must implement robust monitoring and access controls to mitigate these risks.

d. Advanced Persistent Threats (APTs)

Targeted and Stealthy Attacks: APTs involve prolonged and targeted cyberattacks that aim to infiltrate an organization and remain undetected for an extended period. APT actors often have specific objectives, such as data theft or espionage, and use advanced techniques to achieve their goals.

Increased Use of Zero-Day Exploits: APT groups often leverage zero-day vulnerabilities—unknown flaws in software that can be exploited before they are patched—to gain unauthorized access to systems. The use of such exploits highlights the need for organizations to maintain proactive threat hunting and vulnerability management practices.

e. IoT and Smart Device Vulnerabilities

Growing Attack Surface: The proliferation of Internet of Things (IoT) devices and smart technologies has expanded the attack surface for cybercriminals. Many IoT devices have weak security protocols, making them attractive targets for attackers.

Botnets and DDoS Attacks: Compromised IoT devices can be leveraged to form large botnets, which can be used to launch Distributed Denial of Service (DDoS) attacks, overwhelming targets with traffic and causing significant disruptions.

3. New Social Engineering Techniques

a. Phishing and Spear Phishing

Increased Sophistication: Phishing attacks have become more sophisticated, with attackers using social engineering tactics to create convincing emails that trick users into divulging sensitive information or clicking malicious links.

Spear Phishing Campaigns: Attackers are increasingly targeting specific individuals within organizations (spear phishing), using information gathered from social media or other sources to craft personalized messages that appear legitimate.

b. Business Email Compromise (BEC)

Financial Exploitation: BEC scams involve attackers impersonating high-level executives to trick employees into transferring funds or sensitive information. These attacks exploit trust and authority within organizations, leading to significant financial losses.

Ongoing Threat: BEC remains a persistent threat, as attackers continually adapt their tactics to exploit vulnerabilities in email communication and business processes.

4. Implications for Organizations

The emergence of these threats necessitates a proactive and adaptive approach to cybersecurity. Organizations must recognize that traditional security measures may not suffice in the face of increasingly sophisticated attacks. The following implications highlight the need for comprehensive strategies:

a. Enhanced Threat Intelligence

Proactive Monitoring: Organizations should invest in threat intelligence solutions that provide insights into emerging threats, allowing them to stay informed about evolving tactics and vulnerabilities.

Collaboration and Sharing: Engaging in information-sharing initiatives with industry peers, government agencies, and cybersecurity organizations can enhance collective defenses against emerging threats.

b. Comprehensive Incident Response Plans

Preparedness for Ransomware: Organizations must develop and regularly test incident response plans that address ransomware scenarios, including strategies for negotiation, recovery, and communication with stakeholders.

Adaptation to New Threats: Incident response plans should be adaptable to address new and evolving threats, ensuring that organizations can respond effectively in the face of unexpected attacks.

c. Continuous Security Training

Employee Awareness Programs: Ongoing security training and awareness programs are essential for educating employees about emerging threats and best practices for identifying and mitigating risks.

Phishing Simulations: Conducting regular phishing simulations can help organizations assess employee awareness and resilience against social engineering attacks, enabling targeted training interventions.

Emerging threats represent a significant challenge for organizations, requiring continuous adaptation and vigilance in the face of an ever-changing cybersecurity landscape. By staying informed about the latest trends in cyber threats, organizations can proactively strengthen their defenses, enhance incident response capabilities, and foster a culture of security awareness among employees. As cybercriminals become increasingly sophisticated in their tactics, a proactive approach to threat detection and mitigation is essential for safeguarding organizational assets and maintaining trust in an interconnected digital world.

Chapter 4: Setting Up a Threat Hunting Program

In this chapter, we will focus on the essential steps required to establish a successful threat hunting program within an organization. Beginning with a thorough assessment of your organization's unique needs and resources, we will discuss how to identify critical assets, understand existing vulnerabilities, and set clear objectives for your threat hunting efforts. We will then outline the process of creating a comprehensive threat hunting framework that encompasses policies, procedures, and workflows designed to guide your team in their hunting activities. Additionally, we will emphasize the importance of building a culture of security awareness, fostering collaboration across departments, and ensuring that all stakeholders understand their roles in the threat hunting process. By the end of this chapter, you will have a solid foundation for developing a robust threat hunting program, empowering your organization to proactively detect and mitigate cyber threats before they escalate into serious incidents.

4.1 Identifying Organizational Needs and Resources

Setting up a successful threat hunting program requires a thorough understanding of the specific needs and resources of an organization. Before embarking on this journey, it is crucial to assess the unique security landscape of the organization, including existing capabilities, vulnerabilities, and areas for improvement. This chapter will guide organizations through the process of identifying their needs and resources, ensuring that they can develop a tailored threat hunting program that aligns with their strategic objectives.

1. Understanding Organizational Context

a. Business Objectives and Risk Tolerance

Alignment with Business Goals: Threat hunting initiatives should be aligned with the overall business objectives of the organization. Understanding how cybersecurity impacts the organization's goals, such as customer trust, regulatory compliance, and operational continuity, is essential for prioritizing threat hunting activities.

Defining Risk Tolerance: Each organization has a unique risk tolerance that influences its approach to threat hunting. Leadership must establish a clear understanding of the acceptable level of risk and the potential consequences of cyber threats, which will guide resource allocation and strategic planning.

b. Organizational Structure and Culture

Hierarchical Considerations: The organizational structure plays a vital role in the development of a threat hunting program. Understanding how security functions integrate within the organization can help identify key stakeholders, decision-makers, and potential challenges to implementation.

Culture of Security Awareness: A culture that prioritizes security at all levels of the organization will facilitate the success of threat hunting efforts. Organizations should assess their current security culture and identify areas for improvement, such as training and communication strategies to enhance awareness among employees.

2. Assessing Existing Security Posture

a. Current Security Measures

Inventory of Security Tools: Organizations should conduct a comprehensive inventory of their existing security tools and technologies, including firewalls, intrusion detection systems, endpoint protection, and security information and event management (SIEM) solutions. Understanding the capabilities and limitations of these tools is crucial for identifying gaps in coverage.

Evaluating Effectiveness: Assessing the effectiveness of current security measures is essential to identify areas that require enhancement. Organizations can perform security assessments, penetration testing, and vulnerability assessments to evaluate their current posture against industry standards and best practices.

b. Incident Response Capabilities

Existing Incident Response Plans: Reviewing the organization's current incident response plans helps identify how effectively they can respond to security incidents, including ransomware attacks or data breaches. This assessment will inform the development of threat hunting strategies that integrate seamlessly with existing response efforts.

Experience and Skill Levels: Assessing the skill levels of the security team and their experience with threat hunting methodologies will highlight training needs and potential gaps in expertise. Organizations should identify staff who possess the necessary skills or are eager to develop them for effective threat hunting.

3. Identifying Data Sources and Threat Intelligence

a. Data Collection Capabilities

Identifying Critical Data Sources: Threat hunting relies heavily on data. Organizations should identify critical data sources, such as network logs, endpoint data, application logs, and threat intelligence feeds, that can provide valuable insights for threat hunting efforts.

Data Integration: Understanding how data is collected, stored, and analyzed within the organization is essential. Organizations should evaluate their ability to integrate data from disparate sources into a unified platform for efficient analysis and detection.

b. Threat Intelligence Resources

Internal and External Threat Intelligence: Organizations should assess their access to internal threat intelligence, such as historical incident data and contextual information, as well as external sources, including threat feeds and industry reports. This intelligence is vital for understanding the threat landscape and informing threat hunting activities.

Collaboration with Partners: Engaging with industry partners, government agencies, and information-sharing groups can enhance access to valuable threat intelligence. Organizations should explore collaborative opportunities to enrich their threat intelligence capabilities.

4. Defining Goals and Metrics for Success

a. Establishing Clear Objectives

Setting Specific Goals: Organizations should define specific, measurable, achievable, relevant, and time-bound (SMART) goals for their threat hunting program. These goals should align with organizational priorities and address identified vulnerabilities, ensuring a focused and effective approach.

Prioritizing Threats: Organizations need to prioritize the threats they aim to address through threat hunting efforts. This prioritization should be based on factors such as the potential impact on the organization, the likelihood of occurrence, and the organization's risk tolerance.

b. Developing Metrics for Evaluation

Key Performance Indicators (KPIs): Establishing KPIs is essential for evaluating the success of the threat hunting program. Metrics may include the number of threats detected, the time taken to respond to incidents, the effectiveness of threat detection tools, and overall improvements in security posture.

Continuous Improvement: Organizations should incorporate mechanisms for continuous feedback and improvement into their threat hunting program. Regular assessments of performance against established metrics will help identify areas for enhancement and inform future initiatives.

5. Resource Allocation and Budgeting

a. Assessing Resource Requirements

Human Resources: Organizations should evaluate their staffing needs for effective threat hunting. This includes identifying current staff with relevant skills, determining the need for additional personnel, and considering the potential for outsourcing certain functions to third-party experts.

Technology Investments: Assessing the technological resources required for threat hunting is essential. Organizations may need to invest in advanced analytics tools, machine learning algorithms, and threat intelligence platforms to enhance their capabilities.

b. Budgeting for Threat Hunting Initiatives

Cost-Benefit Analysis: Organizations should conduct a cost-benefit analysis to justify investments in threat hunting resources. This analysis should consider potential cost savings associated with risk mitigation, reduced incident response times, and minimized losses from cyber incidents.

Long-Term Financial Commitment: Threat hunting is not a one-time initiative but a continuous process that requires ongoing investment. Organizations should develop a long-term budgeting strategy that accounts for training, technology upgrades, and personnel costs.

Identifying organizational needs and resources is a critical step in establishing a successful threat hunting program. By understanding their unique context, assessing existing security postures, and defining clear objectives, organizations can develop a tailored approach that aligns with their strategic goals. Moreover, a thorough analysis of resource requirements and a commitment to continuous improvement will ensure that threat hunting initiatives remain effective in the face of an evolving threat landscape. By taking these steps, organizations will be better equipped to enhance their cybersecurity posture and proactively address emerging threats.

4.2 Creating a Threat Hunting Framework

Creating a robust threat hunting framework is essential for organizations aiming to enhance their cybersecurity posture and proactively detect and mitigate potential threats. A well-structured framework not only guides the threat hunting process but also ensures that efforts are aligned with organizational objectives and effectively leverage available resources. This chapter outlines the key components of a threat hunting framework, offering a systematic approach to developing and implementing a successful threat hunting program.

1. Establishing a Threat Hunting Team

a. Defining Roles and Responsibilities

Team Composition: The effectiveness of a threat hunting program hinges on assembling a diverse team of cybersecurity professionals with varying skills and expertise. Key roles may include threat hunters, incident responders, data analysts, and threat intelligence analysts.

Clear Responsibilities: Clearly defining the responsibilities of each team member is crucial to streamline operations and ensure accountability. Establishing roles such as lead threat hunter, data analyst, and incident response coordinator helps clarify expectations and enhances collaboration.

b. Fostering a Collaborative Environment

Interdisciplinary Collaboration: Threat hunting requires collaboration across various teams, including IT, security operations, and incident response. Fostering an environment that encourages knowledge sharing and teamwork can enhance the effectiveness of threat hunting efforts.

Continuous Communication: Implementing regular communication channels, such as team meetings and progress reports, facilitates the sharing of insights and findings, enabling the team to adapt quickly to emerging threats and challenges.

2. Developing a Threat Hunting Methodology

a. The Hypothesis-Driven Approach

Formulating Hypotheses: A hypothesis-driven approach involves creating specific hypotheses about potential threats based on existing data, threat intelligence, and organizational context. This method helps focus threat hunting efforts on relevant risks and improves the likelihood of detecting malicious activities.

Testing and Validation: Once hypotheses are formulated, the threat hunting team should actively test and validate them through data analysis, log reviews, and system monitoring. This iterative process refines hypotheses based on findings, allowing for ongoing adjustments to hunting strategies.

b. Incorporating the Cyber Kill Chain

Framework Integration: The Cyber Kill Chain model provides a structured approach to understanding the stages of an attack, from initial reconnaissance to execution. Integrating this model into the threat hunting framework helps hunters identify indicators of compromise (IOCs) and potential attack vectors at each phase.

Targeted Hunting: By aligning threat hunting efforts with specific phases of the Cyber Kill Chain, organizations can tailor their strategies to focus on the most relevant attack techniques and tactics employed by adversaries.

3. Leveraging Threat Intelligence

a. Utilizing Internal and External Threat Intelligence

Gathering Threat Intelligence: Effective threat hunting relies on the integration of internal and external threat intelligence sources. Internal intelligence, such as historical incident data and logs, can inform threat models, while external intelligence from threat feeds and industry reports provides insights into emerging threats and attacker behavior.

Analyzing Threat Data: The threat hunting team should regularly analyze and contextualize threat intelligence to identify patterns, trends, and potential attack scenarios. This analysis enhances the team's ability to anticipate and respond to threats proactively.

b. Threat Intelligence Sharing

Engaging with Communities: Participating in threat intelligence-sharing communities, such as Information Sharing and Analysis Centers (ISACs) or industry-specific groups, allows organizations to gain valuable insights and collaborate on threat detection strategies.

Incorporating Threat Intelligence into Operations: The threat hunting framework should include mechanisms for integrating threat intelligence into daily operations, ensuring that insights inform detection strategies, incident response plans, and risk assessments.

4. Data Collection and Analysis

a. Identifying Data Sources

Comprehensive Data Inventory: Identifying and cataloging relevant data sources is critical for effective threat hunting. This may include network traffic logs, endpoint telemetry, application logs, and cloud service data. A comprehensive inventory enables hunters to understand the data landscape and access relevant information during investigations.

Prioritizing Critical Data: Organizations should prioritize the collection of critical data sources that provide insights into user behavior, system activities, and network traffic. Prioritization ensures that hunters have access to the most pertinent information for threat detection.

b. Advanced Analytics and Tools

Utilizing Security Information and Event Management (SIEM): Implementing a SIEM solution allows organizations to aggregate, analyze, and correlate data from various sources in real-time. SIEM tools enhance visibility into network activities and support proactive threat hunting efforts.

Employing Machine Learning and Behavioral Analytics: Advanced analytics techniques, such as machine learning and behavioral analysis, can identify anomalies and potential threats within the data. These techniques help automate the detection process and reduce the manual effort required by threat hunters.

5. Establishing Metrics and Reporting

a. Defining Key Performance Indicators (KPIs)

Measuring Success: Establishing KPIs is essential for evaluating the effectiveness of the threat hunting program. Metrics may include the number of threats detected, time to detection, and the percentage of validated hypotheses. Defining these metrics helps assess the impact of threat hunting efforts and informs continuous improvement.

Regular Reporting: Implementing regular reporting mechanisms allows the threat hunting team to communicate findings, progress, and metrics to stakeholders. This transparency fosters support for the program and facilitates informed decision-making regarding resource allocation and strategic priorities.

b. Continuous Improvement

Feedback Loops: Incorporating feedback loops into the threat hunting framework enables teams to learn from experiences and adapt their strategies. Regularly reviewing performance metrics and lessons learned from incidents enhances the overall effectiveness of the program.

Training and Development: Ongoing training and professional development are essential for threat hunters to stay updated on emerging threats, tools, and techniques. Providing opportunities for continuous learning ensures that the team remains agile and capable of addressing evolving challenges.

6. Incident Response Integration

a. Collaboration with Incident Response Teams

Seamless Coordination: Threat hunting should be closely integrated with incident response efforts to ensure a coordinated approach to detecting and mitigating threats. Establishing clear communication channels between these teams enhances the overall response to security incidents.

Playbook Development: Developing incident response playbooks that incorporate threat hunting insights helps ensure that response efforts are informed by real-time threat intelligence and contextual analysis.

b. Post-Incident Analysis

Conducting Post-Mortem Reviews: After a security incident, conducting post-mortem reviews helps identify lessons learned and areas for improvement. Analyzing the effectiveness of threat hunting efforts during the incident informs future strategies and enhances preparedness.

Adjusting Threat Hunting Strategies: Insights gained from post-incident analyses should be used to refine threat hunting methodologies, ensuring that the framework evolves in response to real-world experiences and emerging threats.

Creating a threat hunting framework is a critical step for organizations looking to enhance their cybersecurity defenses. By establishing a dedicated threat hunting team, developing a comprehensive methodology, leveraging threat intelligence, and integrating data collection and analysis, organizations can proactively detect and mitigate threats. Establishing clear metrics, fostering collaboration with incident response teams, and committing to continuous improvement are essential for ensuring the long-term success of the threat hunting program. With a well-structured framework in place, organizations will be better equipped to navigate the evolving threat landscape and protect their critical assets from cyber adversaries.

4.3 Building a Culture of Security Awareness

Creating a culture of security awareness within an organization is a vital component of an effective threat hunting program. Employees are often the first line of defense against cyber threats, and fostering a culture that prioritizes security can significantly enhance the organization's overall security posture. This chapter discusses strategies for building a culture of security awareness, emphasizing the importance of education, communication, and engagement at all levels of the organization.

1. Understanding the Importance of Security Awareness

a. The Human Element in Cybersecurity

The Weakest Link: Despite advanced security technologies, human error remains a leading cause of security breaches. Employees may inadvertently compromise security through actions such as clicking on phishing links, mishandling sensitive information, or neglecting to follow established protocols.

Empowerment Through Awareness: By fostering a culture of security awareness, organizations empower employees to recognize and respond to potential threats effectively. An informed workforce is less likely to fall victim to social engineering tactics and other malicious activities.

b. Aligning Security with Organizational Goals

Business Integration: A security-aware culture aligns cybersecurity initiatives with broader business objectives, emphasizing that security is not just an IT issue but a shared responsibility across the organization.

Risk Mitigation: Enhancing security awareness among employees helps mitigate risks, protecting the organization's reputation, financial resources, and customer trust.

2. Leadership Commitment and Support

a. Role of Leadership in Security Culture

Visible Commitment: Leadership plays a critical role in establishing a culture of security awareness. When executives demonstrate a commitment to security through their actions and decisions, it sends a strong message to employees about the importance of cybersecurity.

Resource Allocation: Leaders should allocate appropriate resources for security awareness initiatives, including training programs, communication tools, and technological solutions that reinforce security practices.

b. Establishing Security as a Core Value

Integration into Mission and Vision: Organizations should integrate security into their mission and vision statements, highlighting its importance as a core value. This integration helps employees understand that security is fundamental to the organization's success.

Recognition of Security Efforts: Recognizing and rewarding employees who contribute to security initiatives reinforces the idea that security is everyone's responsibility. Positive reinforcement encourages ongoing engagement and participation.

3. Developing Comprehensive Security Training Programs

a. Tailored Training Initiatives

Understanding Audience Needs: Security training should be tailored to meet the diverse needs of employees across different roles and departments. For example, training for IT personnel may focus on technical skills, while training for non-technical staff may emphasize awareness of social engineering tactics.

Regular Training Updates: Cyber threats are constantly evolving, making it essential to provide regular training updates. Organizations should schedule ongoing training sessions to address emerging threats and reinforce key concepts.

b. Interactive Learning Approaches

Engaging Formats: Utilizing interactive learning formats, such as workshops, simulations, and hands-on exercises, can enhance the effectiveness of security training. Engaging employees in active learning helps reinforce their understanding and retention of security concepts.

Gamification: Incorporating gamification elements, such as quizzes, competitions, and rewards for participation, can make security training more enjoyable and encourage employees to engage actively in the learning process.

4. Communication and Awareness Campaigns

a. Regular Communication Channels

Consistent Messaging: Organizations should establish consistent communication channels to share security-related information, updates, and best practices. Regular emails, newsletters, or intranet updates can keep security top of mind for employees.

Incident Alerts and Lessons Learned: Communicating about security incidents, even minor ones, and sharing lessons learned reinforces the importance of vigilance and provides practical examples of potential threats.

b. Security Awareness Campaigns

Thematic Campaigns: Implementing thematic security awareness campaigns can help draw attention to specific topics, such as phishing prevention, password security, or safe browsing practices. These campaigns can include posters, informational videos, and interactive quizzes.

Security Awareness Month: Organizations can designate specific months or weeks to focus on security awareness initiatives. During this time, they can hold events, workshops, and training sessions to engage employees and promote security practices.

5. Engaging Employees in Security Practices

a. Encouraging Reporting of Security Incidents

Establishing Clear Reporting Channels: Organizations should create clear and accessible reporting channels for employees to report suspicious activities or security incidents. Encouraging employees to report incidents without fear of repercussions fosters a sense of shared responsibility for security.

Feedback Mechanisms: Implementing feedback mechanisms allows employees to provide input on security policies and practices, helping to identify areas for improvement and increasing buy-in for security initiatives.

b. Involving Employees in Security Initiatives

Security Champions: Appointing security champions within different departments can promote a culture of security awareness. These individuals act as liaisons between the security team and their respective departments, helping to disseminate information and encourage participation in security initiatives.

Cross-Functional Teams: Involving employees from various departments in security-focused projects and initiatives fosters collaboration and encourages diverse perspectives on security challenges.

6. Measuring the Effectiveness of Security Awareness Programs

a. Assessment and Evaluation

Surveys and Assessments: Conducting regular surveys and assessments can help organizations gauge employees' understanding of security concepts and identify areas for improvement. This feedback can inform future training and awareness initiatives.

Tracking Incident Reports: Analyzing the volume and nature of reported security incidents can provide insights into the effectiveness of security awareness efforts. A decrease in incidents related to human error may indicate improved awareness and training.

b. Continuous Improvement

Adapting Programs: Security awareness programs should be dynamic and adaptable, evolving based on the organization's changing needs and the threat landscape. Continuous improvement ensures that programs remain relevant and effective.

Benchmarking Best Practices: Organizations can benchmark their security awareness programs against industry standards and best practices to identify areas for enhancement and ensure they are employing effective strategies.

Building a culture of security awareness is essential for organizations aiming to enhance their threat hunting capabilities and overall cybersecurity posture. By engaging leadership, developing tailored training programs, and fostering effective communication, organizations can empower employees to recognize and respond to potential threats effectively. Encouraging employee involvement, measuring program effectiveness, and committing to continuous improvement are critical for establishing a security-conscious culture that protects organizational assets and mitigates risk. As cyber threats continue to evolve, cultivating a culture of security awareness will be a key driver in ensuring that organizations remain resilient and proactive in their cybersecurity efforts.

Chapter 5: Data Collection and Analysis

In this chapter, we will delve into the critical role of data collection and analysis in effective threat hunting. As cyber threats continue to evolve, the ability to gather and interpret vast amounts of data is essential for identifying potential indicators of compromise (IoCs) and anomalous behavior. We will begin by exploring various data sources available to threat hunters, including log files, network traffic, endpoint data, and threat intelligence feeds, emphasizing the importance of collecting relevant and high-quality data. Next, we will discuss best practices for data visualization and analysis, introducing tools and techniques that can help simplify complex datasets and reveal hidden patterns. Additionally, we will cover methods for anomaly detection, enabling you to differentiate between normal and suspicious activities within your environment. By the end of this chapter, you will gain valuable insights into how to effectively harness data to inform your threat hunting initiatives, allowing for more informed decision-making and proactive threat mitigation.

5.1 Effective Data Sources for Threat Hunting

In the world of cybersecurity, effective threat hunting relies heavily on the availability and quality of data sources. Data serves as the foundation for detecting and mitigating threats, enabling security teams to identify anomalies, track adversaries, and respond to incidents in real-time. This chapter discusses various effective data sources for threat hunting, exploring their significance, types, and best practices for utilization.

1. Understanding the Role of Data in Threat Hunting

a. Data as a Source of Intelligence

Indicators of Compromise (IOCs): Data helps identify IOCs, which are artifacts that suggest a potential breach, such as unusual IP addresses, file hashes, or specific user behaviors. By analyzing IOCs, threat hunters can identify and respond to threats before they escalate.

Contextual Insights: Quality data provides context to the threat landscape, helping security teams understand the nature of the threats they face. This context is crucial for prioritizing threat hunting efforts and developing effective strategies.

b. Importance of Comprehensive Data Coverage

Holistic Perspective: A comprehensive collection of data sources enables a holistic view of an organization's security posture. This perspective helps uncover hidden threats and weak points that might otherwise go unnoticed.

Diverse Threat Landscape: Given the diverse nature of cyber threats, a single data source is rarely sufficient. Leveraging multiple data sources enhances detection capabilities and improves the overall effectiveness of threat hunting initiatives.

2. Types of Data Sources for Threat Hunting

a. Network Traffic Data

NetFlow and Packet Capture: Analyzing network traffic data, including NetFlow records and packet captures, provides insights into data flow patterns, allowing threat hunters to identify anomalies that may indicate malicious activity.

Intrusion Detection Systems (IDS): IDS solutions monitor network traffic for suspicious patterns and behaviors. Analyzing IDS logs helps detect potential intrusions and understand attack vectors.

b. Endpoint Data

Endpoint Detection and Response (EDR): EDR tools collect telemetry from endpoints, including processes, file activities, and registry changes. This data enables threat hunters to investigate endpoint behavior and detect potential threats.

Operating System Logs: System logs from endpoints provide insights into user activities, application events, and system errors. Analyzing these logs helps identify abnormal behaviors that may indicate compromise.

c. Application Logs

Web Server Logs: Web server logs capture user interactions and request patterns, which can help identify suspicious activities, such as unauthorized access attempts or abnormal traffic spikes.

Application Security Logs: Logs from applications provide insights into application behavior and access patterns. Analyzing these logs can reveal vulnerabilities or potential exploitation attempts.

d. Security Information and Event Management (SIEM)

Centralized Data Aggregation: SIEM solutions aggregate data from various sources, including network, endpoint, and application logs. This centralized approach enables comprehensive analysis and correlation of events across the environment.

Real-Time Monitoring and Alerts: SIEM systems provide real-time monitoring and alerting capabilities, allowing threat hunters to respond quickly to potential threats based on predefined rules and anomalies detected within the data.

3. External Data Sources

a. Threat Intelligence Feeds

Commercial and Open Source Feeds: Leveraging external threat intelligence feeds, both commercial and open-source, provides valuable insights into emerging threats, known IOCs, and attacker tactics, techniques, and procedures (TTPs).

Industry-Specific Intelligence: Engaging with industry-specific threat intelligence groups and communities allows organizations to access relevant information about threats that may specifically target their sector.

b. Dark Web Monitoring

Monitoring for Leaked Credentials: Monitoring the dark web for leaked credentials and sensitive information helps organizations stay ahead of potential breaches and address vulnerabilities proactively.

Identifying Targeted Threats: Engaging with dark web monitoring services can provide insights into potential threats targeting the organization, including discussions about planned attacks or sales of stolen data.

4. User Behavior Analytics (UBA)

a. Behavioral Patterns and Anomalies

Establishing Baselines: UBA tools establish baselines of normal user behavior, enabling security teams to identify deviations that may indicate malicious activities, such as account compromise or insider threats.

Detecting Insider Threats: By analyzing user activities across various systems, UBA tools help identify potential insider threats and unauthorized data access.

5. Log Management and Retention

a. Importance of Log Retention Policies

Comprehensive Historical Data: Effective threat hunting requires access to historical data for forensic analysis and pattern recognition. Organizations should establish log retention policies that balance storage costs with the need for historical data.

Legal and Compliance Considerations: Log retention policies should consider legal and regulatory requirements for data retention, ensuring that organizations maintain compliance while enabling effective threat hunting.

b. Centralized Log Management

Aggregating Logs for Analysis: Centralizing log management facilitates easier access to data and improves the efficiency of threat hunting efforts. A centralized approach allows security teams to correlate events across multiple systems quickly.

Streamlining Investigations: A centralized log management system streamlines investigations by allowing threat hunters to search and analyze logs from various sources in one place, reducing response times during incidents.

6. Best Practices for Utilizing Data Sources

a. Regular Data Review and Maintenance

Data Quality Assurance: Ensuring the accuracy and quality of data sources is crucial for effective threat hunting. Organizations should regularly review and update data sources to eliminate stale or irrelevant information.

Removing Redundant Sources: Redundant data sources can create noise and complicate analysis. Periodic assessments of data sources help organizations eliminate redundancies and streamline their threat hunting efforts.

b. Collaboration Between Teams

Cross-Departmental Engagement: Collaboration between different teams, including IT, security, and compliance, enhances data sharing and access. Engaging stakeholders from various departments ensures that all relevant data is collected and utilized effectively.

Building Knowledge Repositories: Establishing knowledge repositories for sharing insights, IOCs, and best practices fosters a collaborative environment and enhances the organization's overall threat intelligence capabilities.

Effective data sources are the backbone of a successful threat hunting program. By leveraging a diverse array of data sources, including network traffic, endpoint data, application logs, and external threat intelligence, organizations can enhance their ability to detect, analyze, and respond to potential threats. Establishing best practices for data management, fostering collaboration among teams, and continuously reviewing and improving data sources will significantly strengthen the organization's overall security posture. As cyber threats continue to evolve, maintaining a comprehensive and effective approach to data utilization will be essential for proactive threat hunting efforts.

5.2 Tools for Data Visualization and Analysis

In the realm of threat hunting, the ability to visualize and analyze data effectively is paramount. With the increasing volume and complexity of cybersecurity data, tools that enable clear visualization and insightful analysis empower threat hunters to detect anomalies, identify patterns, and make informed decisions quickly. This chapter discusses various tools available for data visualization and analysis, highlighting their features, strengths, and how they can be effectively integrated into threat hunting workflows.

1. The Importance of Data Visualization in Threat Hunting

a. Simplifying Complex Data Sets

Clarity and Insight: Data visualization transforms complex data sets into clear, comprehensible visuals, allowing threat hunters to discern patterns, trends, and anomalies that may not be immediately apparent in raw data.

Enhanced Decision-Making: Visual representations facilitate quicker decision-making by providing a clear snapshot of the threat landscape. This ability to quickly assess the situation is crucial in fast-paced environments where time is of the essence.

b. Communicating Findings Effectively

Storytelling with Data: Visual tools enable threat hunters to tell a story with data, presenting findings in a way that resonates with stakeholders. Effective visualizations can help communicate the severity of threats, the impact of incidents, and the effectiveness of security measures to non-technical audiences.

Reporting and Documentation: Data visualization tools streamline the reporting process, allowing threat hunters to generate visual reports that summarize key findings, trends, and recommendations for stakeholders.

2. Key Features of Data Visualization Tools

a. User-Friendly Interfaces

Ease of Use: A user-friendly interface is essential for ensuring that threat hunters can navigate the tool effectively. Intuitive design and accessibility features enhance the user experience, allowing users to focus on analysis rather than struggling with complex functionalities.

Drag-and-Drop Functionality: Many modern data visualization tools offer drag-and-drop functionality, enabling users to create visualizations quickly without extensive training or programming knowledge.

b. Data Integration Capabilities

Multi-Source Integration: Effective visualization tools can integrate data from multiple sources, such as SIEM systems, endpoint logs, threat intelligence feeds, and network traffic data. This capability allows threat hunters to analyze data comprehensively and identify correlations across different datasets.

Real-Time Data Streaming: Tools that support real-time data streaming enable threat hunters to visualize current data flows and quickly identify anomalies as they occur, enhancing the overall effectiveness of threat detection efforts.

c. Customizable Visualizations

Flexible Visualization Options: Customization options allow users to create tailored visualizations that suit their specific analytical needs. Common visualization types include heat maps, scatter plots, bar charts, line graphs, and network diagrams, each serving different analytical purposes.

Interactive Dashboards: Interactive dashboards enable users to drill down into data points for deeper analysis, offering a dynamic way to explore relationships and trends within the data.

3. Popular Data Visualization Tools

a. Tableau

Overview: Tableau is a leading data visualization tool known for its powerful analytics capabilities and user-friendly interface. It allows users to create interactive and shareable dashboards.

Key Features: Tableau supports real-time data visualization, multi-source integration, and a variety of chart types. Its intuitive drag-and-drop interface makes it accessible for users with varying levels of expertise.

Use Case in Threat Hunting: Threat hunters can use Tableau to visualize patterns in security data, such as analyzing login attempts, tracking malware activity, or correlating incident reports.

b. Kibana

Overview: Kibana is an open-source data visualization and exploration tool specifically designed for use with Elasticsearch. It excels in visualizing large volumes of log data.

Key Features: Kibana provides real-time data visualizations, customizable dashboards, and powerful search capabilities. Its integration with the Elastic Stack enhances its functionality for security data analysis.

Use Case in Threat Hunting: Kibana can be used to create visual representations of log data, such as analyzing failed login attempts, detecting unusual access patterns, or tracking changes in network traffic.

c. Grafana

Overview: Grafana is an open-source analytics and monitoring platform known for its rich visualization capabilities and extensive plugin support.

Key Features: Grafana supports multi-source data visualization, real-time monitoring, and customizable dashboards. Its flexibility allows users to integrate various data sources seamlessly.

Use Case in Threat Hunting: Threat hunters can use Grafana to monitor key performance indicators (KPIs), visualize network traffic, and track security metrics over time.

d. Microsoft Power BI

Overview: Microsoft Power BI is a business analytics tool that provides interactive visualizations and business intelligence capabilities. It is widely used in organizations for various data analysis tasks.

Key Features: Power BI allows users to create reports and dashboards from multiple data sources, offering a wide range of visualization options and built-in data modeling capabilities.

Use Case in Threat Hunting: Threat hunters can use Power BI to analyze historical security incidents, visualize trends in threat data, and communicate findings effectively to stakeholders.

4. Integrating Data Visualization Tools into Threat Hunting Workflows

a. Establishing Data Pipelines

Streamlining Data Flow: To maximize the effectiveness of visualization tools, organizations should establish data pipelines that facilitate the seamless flow of data from various sources into the chosen visualization platform. This process may involve data cleansing, transformation, and integration.

Automated Data Updates: Implementing automated data updates ensures that threat hunters have access to the most current information, enabling real-time analysis and quicker response times.

b. Collaborative Analysis and Reporting

Team Collaboration Features: Many visualization tools offer collaborative features that allow teams to work together on analysis and reporting. This collaboration fosters a shared understanding of threats and encourages knowledge sharing among team members.

Regular Reporting Cadence: Establishing a regular reporting cadence helps ensure that stakeholders are kept informed of the organization's security posture, emerging threats, and the effectiveness of threat hunting initiatives.

5. Best Practices for Effective Data Visualization

a. Choosing the Right Visualization Types

Aligning Visualizations with Objectives: Threat hunters should select visualization types that align with their specific objectives. For instance, network traffic analysis may benefit from line graphs or flow diagrams, while incident reports may be better represented with bar charts or pie charts.

Avoiding Information Overload: Simplifying visualizations by focusing on key metrics helps avoid overwhelming stakeholders with excessive information. Clear, concise visuals facilitate quicker understanding and decision-making.

b. Ensuring Data Accuracy and Integrity

Validating Data Sources: Threat hunters should validate the accuracy and integrity of data sources before conducting analysis. Ensuring data quality is critical for generating reliable insights and avoiding misleading conclusions.

Continuous Monitoring and Feedback: Organizations should implement continuous monitoring and feedback loops to assess the effectiveness of visualizations and make necessary adjustments to improve clarity and relevance.

Data visualization and analysis tools play a critical role in the effectiveness of threat hunting efforts. By leveraging these tools, organizations can transform complex data sets into actionable insights, enabling faster detection and response to cyber threats. Through effective integration into threat hunting workflows, adherence to best practices, and collaboration among teams, data visualization tools enhance the overall security posture of organizations. As the cyber threat landscape continues to evolve, the ability to visualize and analyze data effectively will be increasingly important for proactive threat hunting and incident response efforts.

5.3 Techniques for Anomaly Detection in Data

Anomaly detection is a critical component of threat hunting, allowing security teams to identify unusual patterns or behaviors that may indicate potential threats or breaches. As cyber threats become more sophisticated, the ability to detect anomalies in large volumes of data is essential for early detection and response. This chapter explores various techniques for anomaly detection in data, discussing their strengths, weaknesses, and best practices for implementation in threat hunting efforts.

1. Understanding Anomaly Detection

a. Definition of Anomalies

- **Types of Anomalies**: Anomalies can be categorized into three main types:
- **Point Anomalies**: Individual data points that deviate significantly from the rest of the dataset (e.g., an unusually high number of failed login attempts from a specific IP address).
- **Contextual Anomalies**: Data points that are normal in some contexts but anomalous in others (e.g., a user accessing sensitive files outside of regular business hours).
- **Collective Anomalies**: A set of data points that together indicate an anomaly, even if individual points may not appear abnormal (e.g., a series of login attempts from different geographical locations within a short time frame).

b. Importance of Anomaly Detection in Threat Hunting

Early Detection: Anomaly detection enables organizations to identify potential threats before they escalate into significant security incidents, allowing for timely intervention and response.

Reducing False Positives: By effectively detecting anomalies, security teams can minimize the number of false positives generated by traditional security systems, focusing their efforts on genuine threats.

2. Techniques for Anomaly Detection

a. Statistical Methods

Z-Score Analysis: Z-score analysis identifies anomalies by measuring the number of standard deviations a data point is from the mean. Points with a Z-score beyond a predefined threshold are flagged as anomalies.

- **Strengths**: Simple to implement and effective for normally distributed data.
- **Weaknesses**: May not perform well with non-normally distributed data or datasets with outliers.

Moving Average and Exponential Smoothing: These techniques analyze time-series data to detect anomalies by comparing current values against historical averages. Anomalies are identified when data points fall outside a specified range of the average.

- **Strengths**: Effective for detecting anomalies in time-series data and adaptable to different data patterns.
- **Weaknesses**: Can lag in real-time detection and may require parameter tuning for optimal performance.

b. Machine Learning Techniques

Supervised Learning: Supervised learning techniques involve training models on labeled datasets, where anomalies are predefined. Common algorithms include:

Support Vector Machines (SVM): SVM can be used for binary classification of normal versus anomalous data.

Decision Trees and Random Forests: These algorithms can classify data points based on features that distinguish normal behavior from anomalies.

Strengths: High accuracy when sufficient labeled data is available.

Weaknesses: Requires labeled datasets, which can be difficult to obtain in cybersecurity contexts.

Unsupervised Learning: Unsupervised learning techniques identify anomalies in unlabeled datasets. Common methods include:

Clustering Algorithms (e.g., K-Means, DBSCAN): These algorithms group similar data points, with points that do not fit into any cluster identified as anomalies.

Isolation Forest: This ensemble method builds decision trees to isolate observations, effectively identifying anomalies based on their separation from the majority of the data.

Strengths: No need for labeled data, making it applicable to a broader range of scenarios.

Weaknesses: May require extensive parameter tuning and can be sensitive to the choice of features.

c. Rule-Based Detection

Heuristic Rules: Organizations can develop heuristic rules based on known behaviors and patterns. For instance, a rule may flag an anomaly if a user attempts to access a large number of files in a short period or logs in from multiple locations within a specific timeframe.

- **Strengths**: Easy to implement and can be tailored to specific organizational needs.
- **Weaknesses**: Rules can become outdated quickly, and over-reliance on static rules may lead to missed anomalies.

d. Ensemble Techniques

Combining Multiple Approaches: Ensemble techniques combine multiple anomaly detection methods to enhance detection accuracy. For example, a system might integrate statistical methods, machine learning models, and heuristic rules to produce a more robust detection mechanism.

- **Strengths**: Increases overall detection accuracy by leveraging the strengths of various techniques.
- **Weaknesses**: More complex to implement and may require additional computational resources.

3. Implementing Anomaly Detection in Threat Hunting

a. Feature Selection and Engineering

Identifying Relevant Features: Selecting the right features for analysis is critical for effective anomaly detection. Features may include user behavior metrics, network traffic patterns, and system log attributes.

Feature Engineering: Transforming raw data into meaningful features can enhance the detection process. For instance, calculating the frequency of logins, login locations, and access times can provide valuable insights into normal versus anomalous behavior.

b. Setting Thresholds and Parameters

Determining Thresholds: Setting appropriate thresholds for anomaly detection algorithms is essential. Too strict thresholds may result in excessive false positives, while too lenient thresholds can lead to missed anomalies.

Adaptive Thresholding: Implementing adaptive thresholding techniques can help adjust thresholds dynamically based on changes in data patterns and user behaviors over time.

c. Continuous Monitoring and Feedback Loops

Real-Time Monitoring: Continuously monitoring data in real-time allows for immediate detection of anomalies as they occur, facilitating prompt investigation and response.

Feedback Mechanisms: Establishing feedback loops helps improve anomaly detection systems. Security teams can review detected anomalies, validate them, and refine detection models based on real-world insights.

4. Best Practices for Anomaly Detection

a. Regularly Update Models and Rules

Model Refreshing: Regularly updating machine learning models and heuristic rules ensures that detection systems remain relevant and effective in identifying new and evolving threats.

Incorporating New Threat Intelligence: Integrating threat intelligence feeds and insights into the anomaly detection process helps organizations stay ahead of emerging threats and adapt detection criteria accordingly.

b. Collaborate Across Teams

Cross-Functional Collaboration: Engaging with teams across the organization, such as IT, security, and compliance, fosters a shared understanding of anomalies and encourages knowledge sharing.

Incident Response Coordination: Coordinating with incident response teams ensures that detected anomalies are promptly investigated and addressed, reducing the potential impact of threats.

Anomaly detection is a crucial aspect of threat hunting, enabling organizations to identify potential threats before they escalate. By employing a variety of techniques, including statistical methods, machine learning, rule-based detection, and ensemble approaches, threat hunters can enhance their ability to detect unusual patterns and behaviors in data. Implementing best practices, such as regular updates, feature engineering, and continuous monitoring, further strengthens anomaly detection capabilities. As the cyber threat landscape continues to evolve, effective anomaly detection will remain a vital component of proactive threat hunting and incident response strategies.

Chapter 6: Threat Intelligence in Hunting

In this chapter, we will explore the pivotal role of threat intelligence in enhancing threat hunting efforts. Threat intelligence provides actionable insights that inform hunting strategies, helping organizations stay one step ahead of potential adversaries. We will begin by defining the various types of threat intelligence—tactical, operational, and strategic—and discuss how each type contributes to the overall understanding of the threat landscape. Next, we will examine the process of gathering and evaluating threat intelligence from both open-source and commercial sources, emphasizing the importance of credibility, relevance, and timeliness. Additionally, we will explore methods for integrating threat intelligence into your hunting workflows, including the development of use cases and hypotheses based on intelligence findings. By the end of this chapter, you will understand how to leverage threat intelligence to enhance your threat hunting capabilities, enabling you to proactively identify and mitigate risks before they materialize into real-world incidents.

6.1 Types of Threat Intelligence: Tactical, Operational, Strategic

In the ever-evolving landscape of cybersecurity, threat intelligence has emerged as a crucial element in an organization's defense strategy. It encompasses the collection, analysis, and dissemination of information regarding current and emerging threats. Understanding the different types of threat intelligence—tactical, operational, and strategic—is vital for organizations to effectively utilize this information for proactive defense measures. This chapter explores each type of threat intelligence, its unique characteristics, and its role in enhancing an organization's security posture.

1. Overview of Threat Intelligence

a. Definition of Threat Intelligence

Threat intelligence refers to the evidence-based knowledge that includes context, mechanisms, indicators, implications, and actionable advice about an existing or emerging threat to assets. It helps organizations understand potential threats, anticipate attack scenarios, and inform decision-making processes.

b. Importance of Threat Intelligence

Proactive Defense: Threat intelligence enables organizations to anticipate and prepare for potential threats rather than merely responding to incidents after they occur.

Informed Decision-Making: By leveraging threat intelligence, organizations can make informed decisions about resource allocation, risk management, and incident response strategies.

2. Types of Threat Intelligence

a. Tactical Threat Intelligence

Definition: Tactical threat intelligence focuses on the immediate and actionable information that aids in the detection, prevention, and mitigation of cyber threats. It often involves specific technical details that can be directly applied to security measures.

Characteristics:

- **Indicators of Compromise (IoCs):** Tactical intelligence includes specific IoCs such as IP addresses, domain names, URLs, and file hashes associated with known threats.
- **Attack Techniques**: It provides insights into the techniques, tactics, and procedures (TTPs) used by threat actors, enabling organizations to implement appropriate defenses.
- **Vulnerability Information**: Tactical intelligence may also include information about specific vulnerabilities in software or hardware that threat actors might exploit.

Examples of Use:

- Security teams use tactical intelligence to update firewalls, intrusion detection systems, and antivirus software with the latest IoCs.
- Organizations may analyze recent malware samples to understand the functionality of a specific threat and adjust their defenses accordingly.

b. Operational Threat Intelligence

Definition: Operational threat intelligence provides a broader view of threat activities and trends over time. It focuses on understanding the context behind threats, including the motivations, capabilities, and behaviors of threat actors.

Characteristics:

- **Contextual Information**: Operational intelligence delves into the who, what, when, where, and why of cyber threats, offering a more nuanced understanding of the threat landscape.
- **Trends and Patterns**: It analyzes trends in cyber attacks, identifying common targets, tactics, and methods employed by attackers.
- **Threat Actor Profiles:** Operational intelligence often includes profiles of threat actors, detailing their capabilities, motivations, and previous activities.

Examples of Use:

- Incident response teams leverage operational intelligence to understand the background of a cyber attack and anticipate the next moves of an adversary.
- Organizations may use operational intelligence to identify emerging threats relevant to their industry or geographical region, enabling them to adapt their defenses accordingly.

c. Strategic Threat Intelligence

Definition: Strategic threat intelligence focuses on the high-level implications of threats and their potential impact on an organization's long-term objectives. It helps inform executive decision-making and long-term security planning.

Characteristics:

- **Business Impact Analysis**: Strategic intelligence assesses the potential impact of cyber threats on business operations, reputation, and financial performance.
- **Risk Assessment**: It aids in understanding the strategic risks associated with cyber threats and helps prioritize security investments.
- **Long-Term Trends**: Strategic intelligence identifies long-term trends in cyber threats, regulatory changes, and emerging technologies that may influence an organization's risk landscape.

Examples of Use:

- Executives and board members use strategic intelligence to understand the broader implications of cybersecurity risks on business objectives and to justify investments in security initiatives.

- Organizations may develop long-term security strategies based on insights gained from strategic threat intelligence, such as identifying critical assets to protect and prioritizing security initiatives.

3. Integrating Threat Intelligence into Security Operations

a. Data Collection and Analysis

Sources of Threat Intelligence: Organizations can gather threat intelligence from various sources, including open-source intelligence (OSINT), commercial threat intelligence feeds, industry partnerships, and government advisories.

Data Enrichment: Enriching collected data with contextual information can enhance its usefulness, enabling security teams to make informed decisions based on a comprehensive understanding of threats.

b. Collaboration and Information Sharing

Collaborative Efforts: Engaging in information-sharing initiatives with industry peers, Information Sharing and Analysis Centers (ISACs), and government agencies can enhance the quality and relevance of threat intelligence.

Feedback Mechanisms: Establishing feedback loops allows organizations to share insights from incidents and adjust their threat intelligence strategies based on real-world experiences.

4. Best Practices for Utilizing Threat Intelligence

a. Aligning Threat Intelligence with Business Goals

Risk-Based Approach: Organizations should align their threat intelligence efforts with their specific risk profiles and business objectives, ensuring that the intelligence gathered is relevant and actionable.

Prioritization: Focusing on threats that pose the greatest risk to the organization enables security teams to allocate resources effectively and address critical vulnerabilities.

b. Continuous Improvement

Regular Review and Update: Threat intelligence programs should be regularly reviewed and updated to adapt to the evolving threat landscape and organizational needs.

Training and Awareness: Ensuring that security personnel are well-trained in utilizing threat intelligence and understanding its implications enhances the effectiveness of security operations.

Understanding the different types of threat intelligence—tactical, operational, and strategic—is essential for organizations looking to enhance their cybersecurity posture. Each type serves a unique purpose, from providing actionable insights for immediate defense measures to informing long-term strategic planning. By integrating threat intelligence into security operations and aligning it with business goals, organizations can proactively address threats, improve incident response capabilities, and ultimately strengthen their resilience against cyber adversaries. In an era of ever-evolving threats, leveraging comprehensive threat intelligence is not just a best practice; it is a necessity for effective cybersecurity management.

6.2 Evaluating Threat Intelligence Sources

In an age where cyber threats are increasingly sophisticated, the demand for accurate and timely threat intelligence has surged. However, the sheer volume of available data can overwhelm security teams, making it crucial to evaluate the reliability and relevance of various threat intelligence sources. This chapter outlines the criteria for assessing threat intelligence sources and provides guidance on how to choose the most effective resources for your organization's needs.

1. Overview of Threat Intelligence Sources

a. Definition of Threat Intelligence Sources

Threat intelligence sources are repositories or providers of information that offer insights into potential threats, vulnerabilities, and adversary behavior. These sources can range from commercial threat intelligence services to open-source platforms, governmental advisories, and community-shared information.

b. Types of Threat Intelligence Sources

Open-Source Intelligence (OSINT): Publicly available information collected from various platforms, such as forums, blogs, and news articles. OSINT is often the first stop for security analysts looking to gather intelligence on current threats.

Commercial Threat Intelligence Feeds: Paid services that provide curated intelligence on emerging threats, including Indicators of Compromise (IoCs), vulnerability data, and threat actor profiles.

Governmental and Regulatory Advisories: Information released by governmental organizations or regulatory bodies that highlight threats and vulnerabilities pertinent to specific industries or regions.

Information Sharing and Analysis Centers (ISACs): Industry-specific organizations that facilitate the sharing of threat intelligence among member organizations, enabling a collective defense against cyber threats.

Community Contributions: Platforms such as GitHub or community forums where security researchers share insights, tools, and findings related to threats.

2. Criteria for Evaluating Threat Intelligence Sources

To effectively evaluate threat intelligence sources, organizations should consider the following criteria:

a. Reliability

Source Credibility: Assess the credibility of the source by checking its reputation in the cybersecurity community. Well-established organizations and reputable analysts are generally more trustworthy.

Track Record: Evaluate the historical accuracy and reliability of the information provided by the source. Consistent, accurate reporting of threats enhances reliability.

b. Relevance

Contextual Fit: Determine whether the intelligence provided is relevant to your organization's specific industry, geographical location, and threat landscape. Intelligence that is highly relevant to your operations is more likely to provide actionable insights.

Customization Options: Some threat intelligence sources allow organizations to tailor the information they receive based on specific needs, enhancing relevance.

c. Timeliness

Frequency of Updates: Evaluate how often the source updates its information. Timely intelligence is crucial for proactively mitigating threats.

Real-Time Alerts: Some sources offer real-time alerts for emerging threats, which can be invaluable for immediate incident response.

d. Depth and Breadth of Coverage

Comprehensive Insights: A good threat intelligence source should provide a broad spectrum of information, including IoCs, threat actor tactics, vulnerabilities, and industry-specific threats.

Focus on Emerging Threats: Sources that track emerging threats and trends offer a more proactive defense strategy, allowing organizations to prepare for future risks.

e. Usability

Ease of Integration: Assess how easily the intelligence can be integrated into your existing security tools and processes. Compatibility with existing systems enhances operational efficiency.

User Interface and Accessibility: A user-friendly interface that allows analysts to quickly access and interpret data can improve overall effectiveness.

3. Sources to Consider

a. Open-Source Intelligence (OSINT) Platforms

Malware Information Sharing Platform (MISP): An open-source threat intelligence platform designed to improve the sharing of structured threat information. MISP allows users to collect, store, and share threat intelligence in a collaborative manner.

ThreatCrowd: A search engine for threat intelligence that allows users to search for information related to IP addresses, domain names, and other IoCs.

CVE Details: A comprehensive database of vulnerabilities that provides detailed information on Common Vulnerabilities and Exposures (CVEs), making it a valuable resource for understanding specific vulnerabilities.

b. Commercial Threat Intelligence Providers

FireEye: Known for its expertise in threat intelligence and incident response, FireEye offers a range of services and reports on advanced threats.

Recorded Future: Provides actionable threat intelligence by analyzing data from various sources and offering insights into threat actor behavior and emerging risks.

CrowdStrike: Specializes in endpoint protection and provides detailed threat intelligence reports that highlight tactics, techniques, and procedures (TTPs) used by adversaries.

c. Governmental Sources

U.S. Cybersecurity and Infrastructure Security Agency (CISA): Offers alerts and guidance on emerging threats, vulnerabilities, and best practices for organizations to improve their security posture.

Europol's Internet Organised Crime Threat Assessment (IOCTA): Provides insights into the latest cybercrime trends and threats affecting Europe, helping organizations understand regional risks.

4. Best Practices for Sourcing Threat Intelligence

a. Cross-Referencing Sources

Multiple Perspectives: Use multiple sources of threat intelligence to cross-reference information. This can help verify accuracy and provide a more comprehensive view of the threat landscape.

Combining OSINT with Commercial Feeds: By integrating OSINT with commercial threat intelligence feeds, organizations can gain a broader understanding of threats and vulnerabilities.

b. Establishing Relationships with Providers

Collaboration: Building relationships with trusted threat intelligence providers can enhance the quality and relevance of the intelligence received.

Feedback Loop: Providing feedback on the usefulness of intelligence can improve the service offered by providers and help tailor future reports to organizational needs.

Evaluating threat intelligence sources is a critical aspect of developing an effective threat intelligence strategy. By considering criteria such as reliability, relevance, timeliness, depth, and usability, organizations can select the most appropriate sources to enhance their security posture. Integrating various threat intelligence sources and leveraging best practices ensures that security teams are equipped with the most accurate and actionable intelligence to proactively defend against cyber threats. As the threat landscape continues to evolve, maintaining a dynamic approach to threat intelligence sourcing will be essential for effective cybersecurity management.

6.3 Sharing and Collaborating on Threat Intelligence

In the constantly evolving landscape of cybersecurity, the ability to share and collaborate on threat intelligence has become paramount. Threat intelligence sharing not only enhances an organization's defense mechanisms but also fosters a collective resilience against cyber threats. This chapter explores the importance of sharing and collaborating on threat intelligence, the best practices for effective information exchange, and the various platforms and initiatives that facilitate collaboration in the cybersecurity community.

1. The Importance of Sharing Threat Intelligence

a. Collective Defense

Strength in Numbers: Cyber threats are increasingly complex and coordinated. When organizations share threat intelligence, they benefit from a broader understanding of attack patterns and can collectively defend against emerging threats.

Mitigating Risks: By sharing information about threats, vulnerabilities, and incident responses, organizations can learn from each other's experiences, thereby reducing the risk of falling victim to similar attacks.

b. Faster Incident Response

Real-Time Intelligence: Collaborative threat intelligence sharing allows organizations to receive timely information about emerging threats, enabling them to respond more rapidly and effectively to incidents.

Early Warning Systems: Sharing threat indicators and intelligence can create early warning systems that help organizations prepare for potential attacks, allowing them to implement preventive measures.

2. Benefits of Collaboration

a. Enhanced Knowledge Base

Diverse Perspectives: Collaboration allows organizations to pool their insights, knowledge, and expertise, leading to a richer understanding of the threat landscape.

Access to Specialized Expertise: Collaborating with external partners, such as industry peers, governmental organizations, or cybersecurity firms, can provide access to specialized knowledge and tools that may not be available in-house.

b. Improved Threat Detection and Analysis

Broader Visibility: By sharing intelligence across organizations, security teams can identify patterns and trends that may not be visible within their isolated environments.

Refining Detection Capabilities: Collaborative efforts can help organizations improve their threat detection mechanisms by validating and refining the indicators of compromise (IoCs) and techniques used by adversaries.

3. Best Practices for Sharing Threat Intelligence

a. Establish Clear Objectives

Define Goals: Organizations should define clear objectives for sharing threat intelligence, such as improving incident response times, enhancing detection capabilities, or mitigating specific threats.

Alignment with Business Needs: Ensure that the sharing objectives align with the organization's overall security strategy and business goals.

b. Create a Structured Framework

Develop Guidelines: Establish guidelines for sharing intelligence, including the types of information to share, the methods of sharing, and the frequency of updates.

Confidentiality and Legal Considerations: Address confidentiality concerns and ensure compliance with legal and regulatory requirements when sharing sensitive information.

c. Use Standardized Formats

Adopt Common Formats: Utilizing standardized formats such as Structured Threat Information Expression (STIX) and Trusted Automated Exchange of Indicator Information (TAXII) can streamline the sharing process and facilitate interoperability among different systems.

Consistent Data Classification: Implement a consistent data classification system to help determine what information can be shared and with whom.

4. Platforms and Initiatives for Threat Intelligence Sharing

a. Information Sharing and Analysis Centers (ISACs)

Role of ISACs: ISACs are industry-specific organizations that facilitate the sharing of threat intelligence among member organizations. They provide a platform for sharing information on threats, vulnerabilities, and best practices, promoting collective defense strategies.

Examples:

- **Financial Services ISAC (FS-ISAC):** Focuses on sharing information among financial institutions to combat threats targeting the financial sector.
- **Healthcare ISAC**: Aims to protect healthcare organizations by providing threat intelligence and collaboration opportunities.

b. Government Initiatives

Cybersecurity and Infrastructure Security Agency (CISA): CISA encourages collaboration between the public and private sectors by offering resources, sharing threat intelligence, and promoting best practices for cybersecurity.

FBI's InfraGard: This program connects private sector members with the FBI to share information related to cybersecurity threats and critical infrastructure protection.

c. Community Platforms

MISP (Malware Information Sharing Platform): An open-source threat intelligence sharing platform designed to improve the sharing of structured threat information among organizations and communities.

ThreatConnect: A threat intelligence platform that enables organizations to aggregate, analyze, and share threat intelligence, helping to create a collaborative defense environment.

5. Challenges in Sharing Threat Intelligence

a. Trust Issues

Building Trust: Establishing trust among organizations is essential for effective collaboration. Organizations may be hesitant to share sensitive information due to concerns about misuse or competitive disadvantage.

Trust Frameworks: Developing trust frameworks that outline how shared intelligence will be used, protected, and attributed can help alleviate these concerns.

b. Information Overload

Managing Volume: The volume of threat intelligence can be overwhelming, leading to information overload. Organizations must prioritize the most relevant intelligence to avoid drowning in data.

Filtering Mechanisms: Implementing filtering mechanisms and automated tools to sift through shared intelligence can help identify actionable insights and reduce noise.

Sharing and collaborating on threat intelligence is crucial for enhancing cybersecurity posture and collective defense against emerging threats. By establishing clear objectives, utilizing standardized formats, and engaging in collaborative initiatives, organizations can improve their incident response capabilities and foster a culture of shared security. While challenges such as trust issues and information overload exist, implementing best practices can help organizations navigate these obstacles. In a world where cyber threats are becoming more sophisticated and widespread, collaborative threat intelligence sharing is not just beneficial—it is essential for organizations seeking to protect their assets and ensure their resilience against adversaries.

Chapter 7: Developing Hypotheses and Hunt Techniques

In this chapter, we will delve into the art and science of developing hypotheses as a foundational aspect of effective threat hunting. A hypothesis-driven approach empowers threat hunters to focus their investigations on specific indicators of compromise (IoCs) and behaviors that suggest malicious activity. We will begin by discussing the importance of formulating clear, testable hypotheses based on threat intelligence and previous incidents, ensuring that your hunting efforts are guided by informed insights. Next, we will explore various hunting techniques, including behavioral analysis, signature-based detection, and advanced analytics, each offering unique advantages in uncovering hidden threats. We will also examine how to apply the MITRE ATT&CK framework to identify potential tactics, techniques, and procedures (TTPs) relevant to your hypotheses. By the end of this chapter, you will have a solid understanding of how to craft effective hypotheses and utilize a variety of hunting techniques to proactively identify and mitigate threats within your organization, enhancing your overall security posture.

7.1 The Importance of Hypothesis-Driven Hunting

Hypothesis-driven hunting is a crucial methodology in the realm of threat hunting that significantly enhances an organization's ability to proactively detect and mitigate cyber threats. This approach emphasizes the importance of forming educated assumptions about potential threats based on existing knowledge and data. In this chapter, we will explore the core concepts of hypothesis-driven hunting, its advantages over traditional threat detection methods, and how it can be effectively implemented within an organization's cybersecurity strategy.

1. Understanding Hypothesis-Driven Hunting

a. Definition of Hypothesis-Driven Hunting

Hypothesis-driven hunting involves the formulation of specific, testable hypotheses regarding potential threats or adversarial activities within an organization's environment. These hypotheses are based on existing threat intelligence, historical incident data, and known attack vectors, guiding security analysts in their search for indicators of compromise (IoCs) or anomalous behaviors.

b. Key Components

Data-Driven: This approach relies on data analysis, where security analysts leverage historical data, logs, and threat intelligence to inform their hypotheses.

Testable Assumptions: The hypotheses should be structured in a way that allows them to be tested through analysis and investigation, making it possible to confirm or refute them based on the evidence gathered.

2. Advantages of Hypothesis-Driven Hunting

a. Proactive Threat Detection

Moving Beyond Signature-Based Detection: Traditional security measures often rely on signature-based detection methods that look for known patterns of attacks. Hypothesis-driven hunting allows organizations to proactively search for threats that may not have been previously identified, enabling them to detect novel attack techniques or variants before they can cause harm.

Anticipating Adversary Behavior: By formulating hypotheses based on observed attacker behaviors and tactics, threat hunters can anticipate potential attack scenarios and identify vulnerabilities in their defenses.

b. Enhanced Focus and Efficiency

Targeted Investigations: Hypothesis-driven hunting allows security teams to focus their efforts on specific areas of concern, reducing the time and resources spent on broader, less-targeted scans for threats.

Improved Resource Allocation: With a clear hypothesis guiding their efforts, security analysts can prioritize their investigations and concentrate on high-risk areas or known vulnerabilities, increasing the overall efficiency of the threat-hunting process.

c. Continuous Learning and Adaptation

Refining Threat Intelligence: As hypotheses are tested and validated (or invalidated), organizations can gather valuable insights that enhance their understanding of the threat landscape, refining their threat intelligence for future hunts.

Building a Knowledge Base: Documenting the hypotheses and the outcomes of investigations contributes to a growing repository of knowledge that can be leveraged in future threat-hunting activities, fostering a culture of continuous improvement.

3. Developing Effective Hypotheses

a. Sources of Information

Threat Intelligence Reports: Leveraging external threat intelligence, including reports from industry peers, security vendors, and governmental advisories, can provide valuable insights into the tactics and techniques used by adversaries.

Historical Incident Data: Analyzing previous security incidents within the organization or industry can reveal patterns and potential vulnerabilities that should be addressed in future hunts.

Anomaly Detection: Utilizing data analytics tools to identify unusual patterns or behaviors in network traffic, user activities, or system logs can serve as a foundation for hypothesis generation.

b. Structuring Hypotheses

Clear and Specific: Hypotheses should be clearly defined and specific enough to guide investigations. For example, rather than stating, "There may be malware on the network," a more precise hypothesis would be, "Recent spikes in outbound traffic from the finance department could indicate exfiltration of sensitive data via malware."

Testable Assumptions: Ensure that hypotheses can be tested using available data. Each hypothesis should include specific indicators or criteria that can be evaluated through data analysis.

4. Implementing Hypothesis-Driven Hunting

a. Collaborative Approach

Cross-Functional Teams: Involving members from various teams—such as incident response, security operations, and threat intelligence—in the hypothesis development process encourages diverse perspectives and insights.

Continuous Feedback: Implementing feedback loops where the outcomes of hypothesis testing are shared with all stakeholders fosters a culture of collaboration and continuous learning.

b. Utilizing Technology

Automation Tools: Employing threat-hunting platforms and automation tools can streamline the hypothesis-testing process, enabling security analysts to efficiently analyze large volumes of data and identify relevant IoCs.

Visualization Tools: Data visualization tools can help security teams to identify patterns and anomalies quickly, supporting the validation or refutation of hypotheses through intuitive graphical representations.

Hypothesis-driven hunting is a powerful approach that transforms threat detection from a reactive to a proactive endeavor. By formulating specific, testable hypotheses based on data and threat intelligence, organizations can enhance their ability to anticipate and respond to cyber threats effectively. The advantages of this methodology—proactive threat detection, focused investigations, and continuous learning—make it a vital component of a comprehensive threat-hunting strategy. As cyber adversaries continue to evolve their tactics, organizations must embrace hypothesis-driven hunting to stay ahead of potential threats and safeguard their digital assets.

7.2 Tools and Techniques for Crafting Hypotheses

Crafting effective hypotheses is a fundamental step in hypothesis-driven threat hunting, allowing security analysts to focus their efforts on identifying potential threats and vulnerabilities within their environment. This chapter explores various tools and techniques that can assist threat hunters in formulating actionable and testable hypotheses, ultimately enhancing their ability to detect and respond to cyber threats proactively.

1. The Role of Tools in Hypothesis Crafting

a. Importance of Automation and Analytics

In the fast-paced world of cybersecurity, the sheer volume of data generated can be overwhelming. Tools that automate data collection and analysis can significantly aid in the hypothesis crafting process, enabling analysts to focus on interpretation rather than mere data handling. By leveraging advanced analytics, organizations can uncover patterns, correlations, and anomalies that inform the development of hypotheses.

b. Integration of Threat Intelligence

Integrating threat intelligence feeds and sources into hypothesis crafting tools can provide real-time insights into emerging threats and vulnerabilities, enabling more relevant and timely hypotheses.

2. Essential Tools for Crafting Hypotheses

a. Security Information and Event Management (SIEM) Systems

Description: SIEM tools aggregate and analyze security data from across an organization's IT infrastructure, providing a centralized view of security events and incidents.

Hypothesis Crafting Applications:

- **Log Analysis**: SIEM systems can analyze logs and identify patterns or anomalies, guiding the formulation of hypotheses related to suspicious activities.
- **Correlation Rules**: Security analysts can create correlation rules within SIEM tools to identify potential indicators of compromise (IoCs) based on known attack patterns.

b. Threat Intelligence Platforms

Description: These platforms aggregate threat intelligence from various sources, including open-source feeds, commercial services, and internal data.

Hypothesis Crafting Applications:

- **Tactical Insights**: Threat intelligence platforms provide insights into specific threat actors, their tactics, techniques, and procedures (TTPs), which can inform the development of targeted hypotheses.
- **Historical Data**: Access to historical threat data allows analysts to recognize trends and patterns that may suggest potential future attacks.

c. Endpoint Detection and Response (EDR) Solutions

Description: EDR solutions provide visibility into endpoint activities, detecting and responding to threats at the device level.

Hypothesis Crafting Applications:

- **Behavioral Analysis**: EDR tools can analyze the behavior of endpoints, highlighting deviations from the norm that can lead to the formulation of hypotheses regarding malicious activity.
- **Automated Responses**: By incorporating automated response capabilities, EDR tools can help validate hypotheses in real-time, enabling rapid action against confirmed threats.

d. Network Traffic Analysis Tools

Description: These tools monitor and analyze network traffic to identify unusual patterns or unauthorized access attempts.

Hypothesis Crafting Applications:

- **Anomaly Detection**: By analyzing network traffic patterns, these tools can help identify deviations that may indicate potential threats, guiding hypothesis development.
- **Protocol Analysis**: Network analysis tools can examine communication protocols to identify suspicious behaviors, informing hypotheses related to data exfiltration or lateral movement within the network.

e. Machine Learning and AI Tools

Description: Machine learning and artificial intelligence tools can analyze large datasets to identify trends, anomalies, and correlations that may not be immediately visible to human analysts.

Hypothesis Crafting Applications:

- **Predictive Analytics**: By utilizing predictive analytics, organizations can identify potential threats before they materialize, allowing for the formulation of proactive hypotheses.
- **Natural Language Processing**: AI tools can analyze threat intelligence reports and security articles, extracting relevant information that can inform hypothesis crafting.

3. Techniques for Crafting Hypotheses

a. Brainstorming Sessions

Collaborative Discussions: Bringing together cross-functional teams for brainstorming sessions can generate diverse ideas and insights, enhancing the quality of hypotheses. Participants can include incident response teams, threat intelligence analysts, and security operations personnel.

Structured Frameworks: Using structured frameworks, such as the "5 Whys" technique, can help teams dig deeper into the reasons behind potential threats and identify underlying factors that may lead to actionable hypotheses.

b. Threat Modeling

Definition: Threat modeling involves identifying potential threats to an organization's assets and determining the most likely attack vectors and methods used by adversaries.

Application: By conducting threat modeling exercises, organizations can create scenarios that outline how attacks may occur, guiding the formulation of specific hypotheses related to those scenarios.

c. Data-Driven Analysis

Exploratory Data Analysis (EDA): Analysts can employ EDA techniques to explore datasets and identify patterns, trends, and anomalies that inform hypothesis development.

Statistical Methods: Utilizing statistical techniques, such as regression analysis or correlation coefficients, can help analysts identify relationships between different variables, leading to the creation of data-driven hypotheses.

d. Use of Frameworks and Methodologies

MITRE ATT&CK Framework: Leveraging established frameworks like the MITRE ATT&CK framework can help analysts categorize and structure their hypotheses based on known adversary behaviors and techniques.

Cyber Kill Chain Model: Using the Cyber Kill Chain model allows organizations to break down the stages of an attack and formulate hypotheses at each phase, improving the likelihood of detecting threats early in the attack lifecycle.

4. Best Practices for Hypothesis Development

a. Be Specific and Testable

Hypotheses should be formulated in a clear, specific manner that makes them testable. For example, instead of stating, "There may be malware on the network," a more precise hypothesis could be, "A recent increase in anomalous DNS queries originating from the finance department indicates the potential presence of malware."

b. Document and Review Hypotheses

Establish a process for documenting hypotheses, including the rationale behind them and the data used to support them. Regularly review and update these hypotheses based on findings from threat hunts and evolving threat intelligence.

c. Create a Feedback Loop

Implement a feedback loop where security analysts can share the outcomes of their hypothesis testing with the broader team. This exchange of information helps refine future hypotheses and contributes to a culture of continuous improvement.

Crafting effective hypotheses is a critical aspect of hypothesis-driven threat hunting. By leveraging a combination of advanced tools and techniques, organizations can enhance their ability to formulate actionable and testable hypotheses that drive proactive threat detection. Utilizing SIEM systems, threat intelligence platforms, EDR solutions, and machine learning tools, combined with collaborative brainstorming, threat modeling, and data-driven analysis, can significantly improve the quality and relevance of hypotheses. As the threat landscape continues to evolve, the ability to craft and validate hypotheses will remain essential for organizations seeking to protect their digital assets and mitigate the risks posed by cyber adversaries.

7.3 Common Hunting Techniques: Behavioral Analysis, Signature-Based Detection

Threat hunting is an essential component of modern cybersecurity strategies, aiming to proactively detect and respond to cyber threats before they cause significant harm. Among the various techniques employed in threat hunting, behavioral analysis and signature-based detection are two of the most widely used. This chapter will explore these two techniques in detail, highlighting their methodologies, advantages, limitations, and best practices.

1. Behavioral Analysis

a. Definition and Purpose

Behavioral analysis involves monitoring and analyzing the actions of users, devices, and systems within an organization to identify patterns or anomalies that may indicate malicious activity. This technique focuses on understanding the "normal" behavior of entities within the environment and detecting deviations from this baseline.

b. Methodologies

Establishing Baselines: The first step in behavioral analysis is to establish baseline behaviors for users, systems, and network traffic. This can include typical login times, file access patterns, data transfer volumes, and application usage. Tools like User Behavior Analytics (UBA) and Network Behavior Analysis (NBA) can be employed to gather this data.

Anomaly Detection: Once baselines are established, security teams can employ anomaly detection algorithms to identify deviations from normal behavior. Anomalies may include:

- Unusual login attempts from unknown locations or at odd hours.
- Excessive data transfers that exceed normal thresholds.
- Access to sensitive files by users who do not typically require such access.

Behavioral Indicators of Compromise (BIoCs): Security teams can develop BIoCs based on observed behaviors associated with previous incidents. For example, multiple failed login attempts followed by a successful one from an unusual IP address may indicate a potential compromise.

c. Advantages of Behavioral Analysis

Proactive Detection: Unlike traditional signature-based methods, behavioral analysis allows for the detection of new and unknown threats that may not have associated signatures.

Contextual Awareness: By understanding normal behaviors, security teams can better contextualize anomalies and respond more effectively.

Reduced False Positives: Behavioral analysis can help reduce false positives by focusing on significant deviations from established baselines rather than relying solely on predefined signatures.

d. Limitations of Behavioral Analysis

Resource Intensive: Establishing baselines and continuously monitoring for anomalies can be resource-intensive, requiring significant computational power and storage.

Complexity: Developing effective behavioral analysis models can be complex, requiring expertise in data analysis and machine learning.

Evasion Techniques: Sophisticated attackers may employ tactics to blend in with normal behavior, making it challenging to detect anomalies.

2. Signature-Based Detection

a. Definition and Purpose

Signature-based detection is a traditional method of threat detection that relies on predefined patterns, or signatures, associated with known threats. These signatures can be based on file hashes, byte sequences, or specific patterns of behavior indicative of malware or malicious activities.

b. Methodologies

Signature Database: Signature-based detection systems utilize a database of known signatures, which is regularly updated based on the latest threat intelligence and incident reports.

Scanning: Security solutions, such as antivirus software and intrusion detection systems (IDS), scan files, network traffic, and system activities against this database to identify potential threats. When a match is found, the system generates an alert or takes predefined actions (e.g., quarantining a file).

Updates and Maintenance: To remain effective, signature-based detection systems require regular updates to their signature databases, ensuring they can detect the latest threats.

c. Advantages of Signature-Based Detection

Speed and Efficiency: Signature-based detection is typically fast and efficient, allowing security solutions to quickly scan and identify known threats.

Low Resource Consumption: Compared to behavioral analysis, signature-based detection often consumes fewer system resources, as it relies on scanning against a set database of signatures rather than continuous monitoring.

High Accuracy for Known Threats: When a signature match is found, it often indicates a high confidence level of compromise, making it an effective method for known threats.

d. Limitations of Signature-Based Detection

Inability to Detect Unknown Threats: Signature-based detection is limited to known threats; it cannot identify new or polymorphic malware that does not have a corresponding signature in the database.

High False Negative Rate: Signature-based systems may miss advanced threats that employ evasion techniques, such as fileless malware or zero-day exploits.

Dependency on Updates: The effectiveness of signature-based detection relies heavily on the timely updating of the signature database, which can be a challenge in a rapidly evolving threat landscape.

3. Combining Behavioral Analysis and Signature-Based Detection

a. Layered Defense Strategy

Both behavioral analysis and signature-based detection have their strengths and weaknesses. A layered defense strategy that combines both techniques can significantly enhance an organization's threat-hunting capabilities. By leveraging signature-based detection for known threats and behavioral analysis for detecting anomalies, organizations can create a more comprehensive approach to threat detection.

b. Integration of Tools

Unified Platforms: Many modern security solutions integrate both behavioral analysis and signature-based detection capabilities, allowing security teams to benefit from the advantages of both methods. Security Information and Event Management (SIEM) systems, for example, can correlate data from various sources and provide a holistic view of potential threats.

Adaptive Response: When both techniques are used together, organizations can implement adaptive response mechanisms. For instance, if a signature match is detected, the system can simultaneously analyze user behavior to assess the context of the alert and determine the appropriate response.

4. Best Practices for Implementing Hunting Techniques

a. Regularly Update Signature Databases

To maintain the effectiveness of signature-based detection, organizations should implement regular updates to their signature databases, ensuring they can detect the latest threats.

b. Establish Baselines for Behavioral Analysis

Developing and maintaining accurate baselines for normal user and system behavior is crucial for effective behavioral analysis. This should involve ongoing monitoring and adjustments based on evolving user behaviors and system configurations.

c. Foster Collaboration Between Teams

Encourage collaboration between security teams to share insights from both behavioral analysis and signature-based detection. This can enhance the overall threat-hunting process and lead to more effective detection and response strategies.

d. Invest in Training and Tools

Organizations should invest in training for security analysts on both behavioral analysis techniques and the effective use of signature-based detection tools. Utilizing advanced tools that integrate both methodologies can also enhance threat-hunting capabilities.

Behavioral analysis and signature-based detection are two fundamental techniques in threat hunting that serve different but complementary purposes. While behavioral analysis allows for the proactive detection of novel threats by identifying anomalies in user and system behavior, signature-based detection excels at quickly identifying known threats through established patterns. By integrating these techniques into a comprehensive threat-hunting strategy, organizations can enhance their ability to detect, respond to, and ultimately mitigate cyber threats in an increasingly complex threat landscape. As cyber adversaries continue to evolve their tactics, the ability to combine and leverage multiple hunting techniques will be essential for maintaining robust cybersecurity defenses.

Chapter 8: Incident Response and Collaboration

In this chapter, we will examine the critical relationship between threat hunting and incident response, emphasizing the importance of collaboration in effectively managing cyber threats. We will begin by outlining the key steps in the incident response process, including preparation, detection, analysis, containment, eradication, and recovery, and how each phase benefits from insights gained during threat hunting activities. Next, we will discuss best practices for fostering collaboration among security teams, IT departments, and management, ensuring a unified approach to incident detection and response. We will also highlight the importance of establishing clear communication protocols and incident escalation procedures to streamline the response process. Additionally, we will explore the value of post-incident analysis, discussing how lessons learned from previous incidents can inform future threat hunting and incident response strategies. By the end of this chapter, you will gain a deeper understanding of how effective collaboration and a well-structured incident response plan can enhance your organization's ability to swiftly identify, contain, and remediate cyber threats, ultimately strengthening your overall security posture.

8.1 Steps in the Incident Response Process

Incident response (IR) is a crucial aspect of cybersecurity that involves a systematic approach to managing and mitigating security incidents. A well-defined incident response process not only helps organizations quickly address threats but also minimizes damage and aids in recovery efforts. This chapter outlines the key steps in the incident response process, providing a framework for organizations to effectively respond to security incidents.

1. Preparation

a. Definition and Importance

Preparation is the foundational step in the incident response process. It involves establishing and equipping an incident response team (IRT), defining roles and responsibilities, and creating an incident response plan. This phase sets the stage for effective incident management when a security breach occurs.

b. Key Activities

Developing an Incident Response Policy: Organizations should create a comprehensive IR policy that outlines the procedures for detecting, responding to, and recovering from security incidents.

Building an Incident Response Team (IRT): Establish a dedicated team with members from various departments (IT, security, legal, communications) to ensure a multi-disciplinary approach to incident handling.

Training and Drills: Conduct regular training sessions and tabletop exercises to prepare team members for real-world incidents, ensuring they understand their roles and the response procedures.

Establishing Communication Plans: Develop communication strategies for internal stakeholders, external partners, and customers to ensure clear and timely information flow during an incident.

2. Identification

a. Definition and Importance

The identification phase involves detecting and confirming that a security incident has occurred. Effective identification is critical, as timely detection can significantly reduce the impact of an incident.

b. Key Activities

Monitoring and Detection: Implement security monitoring tools (e.g., SIEM, IDS/IPS) to continuously analyze logs, network traffic, and endpoint activities for signs of suspicious behavior.

Incident Reporting: Establish clear procedures for employees and stakeholders to report potential security incidents. Encourage a culture of vigilance where staff feel empowered to report suspicious activities.

Initial Assessment: Once a potential incident is reported, conduct an initial assessment to determine the nature and scope of the incident. This may involve analyzing logs, interviewing witnesses, and reviewing system configurations.

3. Containment

a. Definition and Importance

Containment involves taking immediate action to limit the impact of the incident and prevent further damage. This phase is critical to ensure that the incident does not escalate and affect additional systems or data.

b. Key Activities

Short-Term Containment: Implement quick measures to isolate affected systems from the network (e.g., disconnecting compromised devices, disabling accounts) to prevent lateral movement and data exfiltration.

Long-Term Containment: Develop strategies to maintain business operations while addressing the incident, which may involve deploying temporary solutions or rerouting traffic.

Documentation: Record all containment actions taken, as this information will be essential for later analysis and reporting.

4. Eradication

a. Definition and Importance

Once the incident is contained, the next step is eradication, which involves identifying the root cause of the incident and removing all traces of the threat from the environment. This step is crucial to prevent recurrence.

b. Key Activities

Root Cause Analysis: Conduct a thorough investigation to determine how the incident occurred, identifying vulnerabilities or weaknesses that were exploited.

Removing Threats: Eliminate any malware, unauthorized access points, or compromised accounts from the affected systems. This may involve restoring systems from clean backups or applying patches.

System Hardening: Strengthen security controls based on the findings of the root cause analysis. This could include updating security configurations, applying patches, and implementing additional security measures.

5. Recovery

a. Definition and Importance

Recovery involves restoring affected systems and operations to normal functioning while ensuring that the threat has been completely removed. This step is essential for minimizing downtime and restoring business continuity.

b. Key Activities

Restoring Systems: Gradually bring affected systems back online, ensuring that they are free from malware and vulnerabilities. This may involve restoring data from clean backups and validating the integrity of the restored systems.

Monitoring for Recurrence: Implement heightened monitoring and logging for the restored systems to detect any signs of residual threats or recurrence of the incident.

User Notifications: Inform affected users and stakeholders about the recovery efforts and any changes made to security practices.

6. Lessons Learned

a. Definition and Importance

The lessons learned phase involves a retrospective analysis of the incident response process to identify areas for improvement. This step is critical for refining the incident response plan and enhancing future responses.

b. Key Activities

Post-Incident Review: Conduct a debriefing session with the incident response team and relevant stakeholders to evaluate the effectiveness of the response. Discuss what worked well, what didn't, and how the process can be improved.

Updating Incident Response Plan: Revise the incident response policy and procedures based on insights gained from the incident. This may include updating communication strategies, training programs, and technical controls.

Documentation and Reporting: Create a detailed incident report documenting the incident's timeline, response actions taken, and lessons learned. This report should be shared with relevant stakeholders and used for compliance and regulatory purposes.

The incident response process is a vital component of an organization's cybersecurity strategy. By following a structured approach—preparation, identification, containment, eradication, recovery, and lessons learned—organizations can effectively manage security incidents, minimize damage, and enhance their overall security posture. Continuous improvement through post-incident reviews and updates to the incident response plan will ensure that organizations are better prepared to handle future incidents and adapt to the ever-evolving threat landscape.

8.2 Best Practices for Team Collaboration

Effective incident response (IR) is not just about having the right tools and technologies in place; it also heavily relies on strong collaboration among team members and across various departments. A cohesive and well-coordinated response can significantly enhance an organization's ability to manage security incidents efficiently and effectively. This chapter outlines best practices for fostering collaboration within incident response teams, ensuring a comprehensive and unified approach to tackling security incidents.

1. Establish Clear Roles and Responsibilities

a. Define Team Structure

Incident Response Team Composition: Clearly define the roles within the incident response team (IRT), which may include security analysts, incident managers, forensic investigators, legal representatives, and communication specialists. Each member should have specific responsibilities based on their expertise.

Role Clarity: Ensure that all team members understand their individual responsibilities during an incident. For example, security analysts may focus on threat detection, while the incident manager coordinates the overall response.

b. Cross-Functional Involvement

Include Diverse Skill Sets: Encourage collaboration among various departments—such as IT, security, legal, and public relations—to leverage diverse perspectives and expertise during incident response.

Establish Points of Contact: Designate liaisons in each department to facilitate communication and ensure that all relevant stakeholders are engaged during an incident.

2. Foster Open Communication

a. Create a Collaborative Environment

Encourage Open Dialogue: Cultivate a culture where team members feel comfortable sharing information, asking questions, and voicing concerns. Open communication helps prevent misunderstandings and promotes effective teamwork.

Utilize Collaboration Tools: Leverage communication and collaboration tools (e.g., Slack, Microsoft Teams, or dedicated incident response platforms) to facilitate real-time communication during incidents. These platforms allow for quick updates and discussions among team members.

b. Conduct Regular Briefings

Daily Stand-Ups: Implement short daily meetings to provide updates on ongoing incidents, share new information, and address any challenges the team may face. This keeps everyone aligned and informed.

Post-Incident Debriefs: After resolving an incident, hold a debriefing session to review the response process, discuss what went well, and identify areas for improvement. This collaborative reflection is crucial for continuous improvement.

3. Develop a Comprehensive Incident Response Plan

a. Document Procedures

Standard Operating Procedures (SOPs): Create detailed SOPs outlining the steps to be taken during various types of incidents. These should include specific roles and responsibilities, escalation procedures, and communication protocols.

Accessible Documentation: Ensure that the incident response plan and associated documentation are easily accessible to all team members. This can be done using shared drives or collaborative platforms.

b. Regularly Review and Update

Periodic Testing: Conduct regular tests and simulations of the incident response plan to ensure that all team members are familiar with their roles and responsibilities. This also helps identify potential gaps in the plan.

Incorporate Lessons Learned: Update the incident response plan based on insights gained from previous incidents and debriefs to ensure continuous improvement and adaptability.

4. Implement Effective Knowledge Sharing

a. Create a Knowledge Repository

Centralized Knowledge Base: Establish a centralized repository for incident reports, threat intelligence, and lessons learned from past incidents. This resource can be invaluable for training new team members and enhancing the team's collective knowledge.

Documentation Standards: Develop standardized documentation practices to ensure that all incidents are recorded consistently. This will facilitate easier reference and knowledge sharing in the future.

b. Encourage Mentorship and Training

Peer Mentorship: Foster a culture of mentorship within the team, where experienced members support and guide newer team members. This helps build skills and enhances collaboration.

Training Sessions: Organize regular training sessions and workshops to enhance team members' skills in incident response, threat analysis, and relevant technologies. Keeping the team well-informed fosters a collaborative environment.

5. Leverage Technology for Collaboration

a. Utilize Incident Management Tools

Incident Tracking Systems: Implement incident management tools (e.g., Jira, ServiceNow) to track incidents, assign tasks, and monitor progress. These tools help ensure accountability and transparency within the team.

Integrated Communication Channels: Use integrated communication features within incident management tools to streamline communication and collaboration among team members during an incident.

b. Real-Time Monitoring Tools

Dashboards and Reporting Tools: Leverage dashboards that provide real-time visibility into security incidents and their statuses. This allows team members to stay informed and quickly respond to emerging threats.

Automated Alerts: Set up automated alerts for specific incidents or threats, ensuring that the relevant team members are promptly informed and can collaborate on responses.

6. Promote a Culture of Continuous Improvement

a. Encourage Feedback

Open Feedback Channels: Establish channels for team members to provide feedback on processes, tools, and communication methods. Actively seeking input from team members fosters a sense of ownership and encourages collaboration.

Iterative Improvements: Use feedback from team members to iterate on processes and practices continuously, ensuring that the incident response strategy evolves with emerging threats and changing environments.

b. Celebrate Successes

Recognize Team Achievements: Celebrate successful incident responses and acknowledge individual contributions. Recognizing achievements boosts morale and reinforces the value of collaboration.

Share Success Stories: Use successful incident responses as case studies to highlight effective collaboration and strategies within the team, encouraging further engagement and teamwork.

Collaboration is a cornerstone of effective incident response. By establishing clear roles and responsibilities, fostering open communication, developing comprehensive response plans, implementing knowledge-sharing practices, leveraging technology, and promoting a culture of continuous improvement, organizations can enhance their incident response capabilities. A well-coordinated incident response team can respond more efficiently and effectively to security incidents, ultimately reducing the impact of cyber threats and strengthening the organization's overall security posture. As the threat landscape continues to evolve, prioritizing collaboration within incident response teams will be essential for maintaining resilience against cyber threats.

8.3 Post-Incident Analysis and Learning

Post-incident analysis is a critical component of the incident response process that involves reviewing and evaluating the actions taken during a security incident. This phase not only focuses on what occurred during the incident but also aims to extract valuable lessons that can enhance future incident response efforts. By systematically analyzing the incident, organizations can improve their security posture, reduce response times, and better prepare for future incidents. This chapter outlines the steps involved in post-incident analysis, the importance of learning from incidents, and best practices for continuous improvement.

1. Importance of Post-Incident Analysis

a. Understanding the Incident Lifecycle

Post-incident analysis provides insight into the entire lifecycle of a security incident—from detection and response to recovery. This understanding is crucial for identifying weaknesses in existing processes and making informed decisions about future improvements.

b. Identifying Root Causes

One of the primary objectives of post-incident analysis is to identify the root causes of the incident. By understanding what led to the security breach, organizations can address underlying vulnerabilities and prevent similar incidents from occurring in the future.

c. Enhancing Incident Response Plans

The insights gained from post-incident analysis can inform updates to the incident response plan. This continuous improvement loop helps organizations adapt to evolving threats and enhances their overall incident response capabilities.

2. Steps in Post-Incident Analysis

a. Initial Review and Documentation

Gather Incident Data: Collect all relevant data related to the incident, including logs, alerts, incident reports, and communications. This comprehensive data collection is essential for an accurate analysis.

Document the Timeline: Create a timeline of events that occurred during the incident. Documenting the sequence of actions taken, decisions made, and communication exchanges provides a clear picture of the incident's progression.

b. Conduct a Root Cause Analysis (RCA)

Identify Contributing Factors: Analyze the data collected to identify the contributing factors that led to the incident. This may include technical vulnerabilities, human errors, or procedural gaps.

Use RCA Techniques: Employ root cause analysis techniques, such as the "5 Whys" or Fishbone Diagram (Ishikawa), to systematically uncover the underlying causes of the incident. These techniques facilitate deeper exploration of issues and help ensure that the analysis is thorough.

c. Evaluate Incident Response Effectiveness

Assess Response Actions: Review the actions taken by the incident response team during the incident. Evaluate the effectiveness of each step, including detection, containment, eradication, and recovery.

Identify Strengths and Weaknesses: Determine what aspects of the incident response were successful and which areas need improvement. This evaluation should consider response times, coordination, communication, and the use of tools and technologies.

3. Lessons Learned and Recommendations

a. Document Findings

Comprehensive Incident Report: Create a detailed incident report that summarizes the findings from the post-incident analysis. This report should include the timeline of events, root causes, response effectiveness, and lessons learned.

Highlight Key Recommendations: Based on the analysis, outline specific recommendations for improving incident response processes, policies, and technologies. This may include recommendations for training, tool enhancements, or changes to procedures.

b. Share Findings with Stakeholders

Internal Communication: Share the findings of the post-incident analysis with relevant stakeholders, including management, IT, security teams, and affected departments. Ensuring that all stakeholders are informed promotes transparency and fosters a culture of accountability.

External Reporting: If applicable, report the findings to external stakeholders, such as regulatory bodies or customers, especially in cases of data breaches. Clear communication can help maintain trust and compliance.

4. Continuous Improvement

a. Update Incident Response Plans

Incorporate Lessons Learned: Use the insights gained from the post-incident analysis to update the organization's incident response plan. This may include modifying procedures, enhancing communication protocols, and incorporating new technologies.

Adjust Training Programs: Based on the analysis, revise training programs for incident response team members to address any skill gaps identified during the incident. Continuous training ensures that team members remain proficient in their roles.

b. Conduct Regular Drills and Simulations

Tabletop Exercises: Organize tabletop exercises that simulate security incidents to test the updated incident response plan. These exercises help reinforce lessons learned and ensure that team members are prepared to respond effectively.

Evaluate Response Performance: After each drill or simulation, conduct a post-exercise review to evaluate the team's performance and identify areas for further improvement.

5. Building a Learning Culture

a. Foster Open Feedback Loops

Encourage Feedback: Create an environment where team members feel comfortable providing feedback on the incident response process. Open dialogue encourages continuous learning and fosters a collaborative atmosphere.

Recognize Contributions: Acknowledge the efforts of team members who contributed to the incident response. Recognition boosts morale and encourages a culture of learning and improvement.

b. Establish a Knowledge Sharing Mechanism

Knowledge Repository: Develop a centralized repository for incident reports, lessons learned, and best practices. This resource should be accessible to all team members and serve as a reference for future incident responses.

Regular Review Sessions: Schedule regular review sessions to discuss recent incidents, share lessons learned, and refine response strategies. These sessions promote continuous learning and ensure that the team remains vigilant.

Post-incident analysis and learning are essential components of an effective incident response strategy. By systematically reviewing and analyzing incidents, organizations can gain valuable insights that inform their security practices, enhance their incident response capabilities, and reduce the likelihood of future breaches. Emphasizing a culture of continuous improvement, open communication, and knowledge sharing enables organizations to adapt to the evolving threat landscape and build resilience against cyber threats. As security incidents become increasingly sophisticated, the ability to learn from past experiences will be crucial for maintaining a strong security posture and ensuring the organization's long-term success.

Chapter 9: Case Studies in Threat Hunting

In this chapter, we will explore real-world case studies that highlight the practical application of threat hunting strategies and the lessons learned from both successful and failed operations. By analyzing notable incidents, we will illustrate how organizations have effectively employed threat hunting methodologies to detect and respond to cyber threats in a timely manner. Each case study will provide insights into the specific techniques used, the challenges faced, and the outcomes achieved, offering valuable takeaways that can inform future threat hunting initiatives. We will also examine instances where organizations fell short in their threat hunting efforts, identifying key missteps and how they could have been avoided. Additionally, we will discuss the evolving nature of cyber threats and how organizations can adapt their hunting strategies based on insights gained from these case studies. By the end of this chapter, you will have a clearer understanding of how theoretical concepts translate into real-world practice, equipping you with the knowledge to implement effective threat hunting strategies tailored to your organization's unique challenges.

9.1 Analysis of a Successful Threat Hunting Operation

Successful threat hunting operations play a crucial role in identifying and mitigating advanced threats before they can cause significant damage. By proactively seeking out threats, organizations can enhance their security posture and reduce the risk of breaches. In this chapter, we will analyze a successful threat hunting operation, exploring the methodologies used, the challenges faced, and the outcomes achieved. This analysis will provide insights into best practices and highlight the importance of a proactive approach to cybersecurity.

1. Background of the Operation

a. Context and Environment

The organization in focus is a mid-sized financial institution that handles sensitive customer data and transactions. Given the increasing frequency of cyberattacks targeting the financial sector, the organization recognized the need for a robust threat hunting program to safeguard its assets and reputation.

b. Motivation for Threat Hunting

Prior to initiating the threat hunting operation, the organization experienced several minor security incidents, including phishing attacks and unauthorized access attempts. Although these incidents were contained, they highlighted vulnerabilities within the network. To address these concerns, the organization decided to launch a dedicated threat hunting operation aimed at identifying potential threats that traditional security measures might miss.

2. Methodology of the Threat Hunting Operation

a. Establishing a Hypothesis

The threat hunting team began the operation by developing a set of hypotheses based on recent security incidents and emerging threat intelligence. They suspected that advanced persistent threats (APTs) might be targeting their environment, particularly focusing on:

- Unusual login activities from external IP addresses
- Anomalies in user behavior patterns
- Signs of lateral movement within the network

b. Data Collection and Analysis

To validate their hypotheses, the team collected data from various sources, including:

- **Logs**: Security Information and Event Management (SIEM) systems provided logs from firewalls, intrusion detection systems, and endpoint security solutions.
- **Network Traffic**: Network analysis tools helped monitor unusual traffic patterns and identify potential command-and-control (C2) communications.
- **Endpoint Data**: Endpoint detection and response (EDR) tools were used to gather telemetry data from devices within the organization.

Using this data, the team performed the following analyses:

- **Behavioral Analysis**: They analyzed user behavior to identify deviations from normal patterns, such as unexpected access to sensitive data or unusual file transfers.
- **Threat Intelligence Correlation**: The team correlated their findings with threat intelligence feeds to determine if any identified indicators of compromise (IOCs) matched known threats.

c. Identification of Anomalies

During the analysis phase, the threat hunting team discovered several anomalies that warranted further investigation:

- **Suspicious Login Attempts**: Multiple login attempts were detected from an IP address associated with a known threat actor. The logs indicated that the attempts originated from a region with no legitimate business presence.
- **Unusual Internal Activity**: One employee's account exhibited behavior that was inconsistent with their typical activity, such as accessing sensitive files at odd hours and performing unusual file downloads.

3. Response Actions Taken

a. Immediate Containment

Upon identifying the suspicious activities, the threat hunting team quickly took the following containment actions:

- **Account Lockout**: The team locked the compromised employee's account to prevent further unauthorized access.
- **Network Segmentation**: They isolated affected systems from the network to contain potential lateral movement and limit the spread of any possible threat.

b. Forensic Investigation

Following containment, a thorough forensic investigation was conducted to understand the extent of the compromise:

- **Malware Analysis**: The team analyzed endpoints for signs of malware, using tools to identify any malicious binaries or processes.
- **Data Exfiltration Check**: They investigated logs for any evidence of data exfiltration, focusing on large data transfers to external addresses.

c. Collaboration with IT and Legal Teams

Throughout the incident, the threat hunting team collaborated closely with IT and legal teams to ensure compliance with regulations and minimize the impact on business operations. This collaboration included:

- **Communication with Stakeholders**: Keeping key stakeholders informed about the incident status and response actions taken.
- **Documentation for Legal Purposes**: Meticulously documenting all findings, actions, and communications for potential legal ramifications.

4. Outcomes and Lessons Learned

a. Successful Mitigation of Threats

The threat hunting operation ultimately led to the identification of a sophisticated APT that had gained initial access to the organization's network. Thanks to the proactive measures taken, the organization was able to:

- Remove the threat actor's presence from the network.
- Mitigate potential data breaches and protect sensitive customer information.

b. Continuous Improvement

Following the successful threat hunting operation, the organization took several steps to improve its security posture:

- **Refinement of Threat Hunting Techniques**: The team refined its threat hunting methodologies based on the lessons learned during the operation, focusing on enhancing data collection and analysis techniques.
- **Regular Threat Hunting Cycles**: The organization established regular threat hunting cycles to maintain vigilance against evolving threats and strengthen its overall security posture.
- **Enhanced Security Awareness Training**: The incident prompted the organization to implement additional security awareness training for employees, emphasizing the importance of recognizing phishing attempts and suspicious activities.

The analysis of this successful threat hunting operation underscores the importance of a proactive approach to cybersecurity. By establishing clear hypotheses, utilizing robust data collection methods, and responding swiftly to identified threats, the organization was able to mitigate a potentially serious incident effectively. Continuous improvement, collaboration among teams, and an emphasis on security awareness are critical components of a successful threat hunting program. As cyber threats continue to evolve, organizations must remain vigilant and adapt their strategies to effectively combat emerging risks. The insights gained from this operation serve as a valuable reference for organizations seeking to enhance their threat hunting capabilities and improve their overall cybersecurity posture.

9.2 Lessons from a Major Cybersecurity Breach

Cybersecurity breaches can have devastating effects on organizations, leading to financial loss, reputational damage, and regulatory repercussions. Analyzing these incidents provides invaluable insights that can help organizations strengthen their security measures and prevent similar breaches in the future. In this chapter, we will examine a major cybersecurity breach, explore the lessons learned, and discuss how organizations can implement these lessons to enhance their security posture.

1. Overview of the Cybersecurity Breach

a. Background of the Incident

The breach in focus involved a prominent healthcare organization that suffered a significant data breach impacting millions of patient records. The incident was discovered after unusual activity was detected in the organization's network, prompting an internal investigation. The attackers exploited vulnerabilities in the organization's systems, gaining unauthorized access to sensitive patient information, including names, social security numbers, and medical histories.

b. Initial Response

Upon discovering the breach, the organization initiated its incident response plan, which included containment measures, forensic investigation, and communication with affected parties. However, the incident had already caused substantial damage, leading to a loss of patient trust and legal scrutiny.

2. Key Lessons Learned

a. Importance of Proactive Threat Detection

Continuous Monitoring: The breach highlighted the need for continuous monitoring of network activity. The organization lacked adequate intrusion detection and prevention systems, allowing the attackers to operate undetected for an extended period. Organizations must invest in robust monitoring solutions to detect anomalies and respond swiftly to potential threats.

Threat Intelligence Utilization: Leveraging threat intelligence can significantly enhance an organization's ability to identify emerging threats. By staying informed about the latest attack vectors and threat actors, organizations can implement proactive measures to mitigate risks.

b. Strengthening Vulnerability Management

Regular Vulnerability Assessments: The organization failed to conduct regular vulnerability assessments, which allowed known vulnerabilities to be exploited. Conducting routine assessments and penetration testing can help organizations identify weaknesses before attackers do.

Patch Management: A lack of timely patch management contributed to the breach. Organizations should establish a robust patch management process to ensure that software and systems are up to date with the latest security fixes.

c. Enhancing Incident Response Preparedness

Comprehensive Incident Response Plan: The organization's incident response plan was insufficiently detailed, resulting in confusion during the initial response. Organizations must develop comprehensive incident response plans that outline roles, responsibilities, and procedures for various incident scenarios.

Regular Drills and Simulations: Conducting regular incident response drills can help ensure that team members are familiar with their roles and can respond effectively during a real incident. Simulations can also reveal gaps in the response plan that need to be addressed.

3. Communication and Transparency

a. Timely Communication with Stakeholders

Informing Affected Parties: The organization delayed communicating with affected patients, leading to increased frustration and distrust. Transparency is critical during a breach; organizations should promptly inform affected individuals about the incident and the steps being taken to address it.

Regulatory Compliance: Organizations must be aware of their legal obligations regarding breach notification. Compliance with regulations, such as HIPAA in the healthcare sector, is essential to avoid legal repercussions and maintain trust.

b. Engaging External Experts

Collaboration with Third-Party Experts: The organization initially underestimated the value of involving external cybersecurity experts during the incident response. Engaging third-party experts can provide valuable insights and resources to effectively manage the breach and minimize damage.

Public Relations Management: Managing public perception during a breach is crucial. Organizations should have a crisis communication plan in place to address media inquiries and maintain stakeholder confidence.

4. Building a Culture of Security Awareness

a. Employee Training and Awareness

Regular Security Training: The breach revealed gaps in employee security awareness. Organizations should implement regular training programs to educate employees about cybersecurity best practices, social engineering tactics, and how to recognize potential threats.

Phishing Simulations: Conducting phishing simulations can help employees recognize phishing attempts and improve their ability to respond appropriately to suspicious communications.

b. Creating a Security-Conscious Environment

Encouraging Reporting: Organizations should foster an environment where employees feel comfortable reporting suspicious activity. Implementing a clear reporting process can lead to quicker identification of potential threats.

Leadership Involvement: Leadership should prioritize cybersecurity and actively promote a culture of security within the organization. When leaders emphasize the importance of security, employees are more likely to take it seriously.

5. Continuous Improvement and Adaptation

a. Post-Incident Analysis

Conducting a Post-Mortem Review: After addressing the breach, organizations should conduct a thorough post-mortem review to analyze what went wrong, identify weaknesses in the response, and gather insights for future improvements.

Incorporating Lessons Learned: The organization should integrate the lessons learned from the breach into its security policies, incident response plans, and training programs to enhance its overall security posture.

b. Adapting to Evolving Threats

Staying Informed: The cybersecurity landscape is constantly evolving, and organizations must stay informed about new threats and vulnerabilities. Regularly reviewing threat intelligence reports and industry trends can help organizations adapt their security strategies accordingly.

Investing in Security Technologies: Organizations should continually evaluate and invest in new security technologies, such as advanced threat detection solutions and machine learning-based analytics, to enhance their ability to detect and respond to emerging threats.

The lessons learned from major cybersecurity breaches are invaluable for organizations seeking to strengthen their security posture and prevent future incidents. By focusing on proactive threat detection, strengthening vulnerability management, enhancing incident response preparedness, fostering communication and transparency, and building a culture of security awareness, organizations can significantly reduce their risk of breaches. Continuous improvement and adaptation to evolving threats are essential components of a successful cybersecurity strategy. In an increasingly complex threat landscape, organizations must remain vigilant and proactive to protect their assets and maintain the trust of their stakeholders.

9.3 Innovations in Threat Hunting Techniques: A Case Review

As cyber threats continue to evolve in sophistication and complexity, the need for innovative threat hunting techniques has become increasingly critical. This chapter reviews a specific case study of an organization that successfully implemented cutting-edge threat hunting methodologies, highlighting the techniques employed, the challenges faced, and the outcomes achieved. By examining this case, we can glean insights into the innovations in threat hunting that are shaping the future of cybersecurity.

1. Overview of the Organization

a. Background Information

The organization in focus is a global technology firm specializing in software development and IT services. With a large and diverse client base, the company handles sensitive data and critical business operations for various industries. Given its prominent position in the market, it has been a target for cybercriminals, leading to a concerted effort to enhance its threat hunting capabilities.

b. Motivation for Innovation

In the wake of several near-miss incidents that highlighted vulnerabilities in their existing security measures, the organization recognized the necessity of adopting innovative threat hunting techniques. Their objective was to improve detection capabilities, reduce response times, and better defend against advanced persistent threats (APTs).

2. Innovative Threat Hunting Techniques Employed

a. Machine Learning and AI

Predictive Analytics: The organization implemented machine learning algorithms to analyze historical data and identify patterns indicative of potential threats. By leveraging predictive analytics, the threat hunting team could proactively search for anomalies and outliers that might signal malicious activity.

Behavioral Analysis: The use of AI-driven behavioral analysis allowed the organization to establish baseline behaviors for users and systems. Any deviations from these baselines were flagged for further investigation, enabling the team to detect potential insider threats and compromised accounts more effectively.

b. Threat Intelligence Automation

Integration with Threat Intelligence Feeds: The organization integrated multiple threat intelligence feeds into their security systems to automate the process of correlating real-time data with known indicators of compromise (IOCs). This integration enabled quicker identification of threats that matched existing threat actor profiles.

Automated Threat Scoring: An automated threat scoring system was developed to prioritize alerts based on the risk level and potential impact on the organization. This approach helped the team focus their efforts on the most critical threats, improving overall efficiency.

c. Enhanced Visualization Tools

Interactive Dashboards: The organization implemented advanced data visualization tools that provided interactive dashboards for real-time monitoring of network activity. These dashboards allowed the threat hunting team to quickly identify suspicious patterns and trends, facilitating faster decision-making.

Graph Analytics: The use of graph analytics helped the team visualize relationships between various entities within the network, making it easier to spot lateral movement, abnormal connections, and potential attack paths.

3. The Threat Hunting Process

a. Hypothesis-Driven Hunting

The threat hunting team adopted a hypothesis-driven approach, formulating specific hypotheses based on threat intelligence and historical incidents. For example, one hypothesis focused on the possibility of a targeted phishing campaign aimed at employees with access to sensitive data. This approach ensured that their hunting efforts were strategic and focused.

b. Data Collection and Enrichment

To validate their hypotheses, the team collected data from various sources, including:

- **SIEM Logs**: Security Information and Event Management (SIEM) logs provided a wealth of information on user activities, access attempts, and system alerts.
- **Endpoint Data**: Endpoint Detection and Response (EDR) tools were used to collect telemetry data from devices within the organization, helping to identify unusual behaviors.

The collected data was enriched with threat intelligence, providing context that enhanced the team's ability to assess the severity of potential threats.

c. Collaborative Threat Hunting

Recognizing the importance of collaboration, the organization established cross-functional teams that included representatives from IT, security, and incident response. This collaborative approach fostered knowledge sharing and improved the overall effectiveness of threat hunting operations.

4. Challenges Faced

a. Volume of Data

One of the primary challenges faced by the organization was the sheer volume of data generated by its systems. Sifting through massive amounts of information to identify relevant threats proved time-consuming and resource-intensive. The integration of machine learning and automation was crucial in addressing this challenge.

b. Evolving Threat Landscape

The constantly evolving threat landscape posed another significant challenge. Cybercriminals continuously adapt their tactics, making it essential for the organization to stay updated on the latest threats and vulnerabilities. The organization focused on establishing robust threat intelligence partnerships to mitigate this challenge.

5. Outcomes and Impact

a. Improved Threat Detection and Response Times

The implementation of innovative threat hunting techniques resulted in a marked improvement in the organization's threat detection capabilities. The team was able to identify and respond to potential threats much more quickly than before, reducing the average time to detection from weeks to hours.

b. Reduced Incidence of Successful Breaches

Following the adoption of the new techniques, the organization experienced a significant reduction in successful breaches. By proactively hunting for threats, the organization was able to thwart multiple phishing campaigns and thwart advanced persistent threats targeting its network.

c. Enhanced Security Culture

The success of the threat hunting operation fostered a stronger security culture within the organization. Employees became more aware of cybersecurity risks, leading to increased vigilance and a greater willingness to report suspicious activities.

The case review of this technology firm illustrates the importance of innovation in threat hunting techniques in addressing the ever-evolving landscape of cyber threats. By leveraging machine learning, automation, and collaborative approaches, the organization significantly enhanced its threat detection and response capabilities. The lessons learned from this case underscore the necessity for organizations to remain proactive, invest in innovative technologies, and foster a culture of security awareness to effectively combat emerging threats. As the cyber threat landscape continues to change, organizations must be prepared to adapt their strategies and embrace new methodologies in their threat hunting efforts to stay ahead of adversaries.

Chapter 10: Measuring Success in Threat Hunting

In this chapter, we will focus on the critical task of measuring the success of your threat hunting program. Establishing clear metrics and key performance indicators (KPIs) is essential for evaluating the effectiveness of your hunting efforts and demonstrating their value to stakeholders. We will begin by discussing the different types of metrics that can be employed, including operational metrics that track the efficiency of the hunting process and outcome metrics that assess the impact of threat hunting on overall security posture. Next, we will explore various tools and methodologies for tracking performance, including dashboards and reporting frameworks that provide insights into hunting activities and results. Additionally, we will emphasize the importance of continuous improvement, discussing how regular reviews of metrics and KPIs can inform adjustments to hunting strategies and enhance overall effectiveness. By the end of this chapter, you will be equipped with the knowledge to implement a robust measurement framework for your threat hunting program, enabling you to articulate its successes and areas for growth while fostering a culture of accountability and excellence within your security team.

10.1 Establishing Metrics for Threat Hunting

Metrics play a crucial role in evaluating the effectiveness of threat hunting programs. By establishing clear metrics, organizations can assess their threat hunting efforts, identify areas for improvement, and demonstrate the value of their cybersecurity investments. This chapter discusses the key metrics that organizations should consider when establishing a framework for measuring the success of their threat hunting activities.

1. Importance of Metrics in Threat Hunting

a. Driving Continuous Improvement

Establishing metrics enables organizations to track their progress and identify trends over time. By measuring specific aspects of their threat hunting activities, teams can refine their strategies and processes to enhance their overall effectiveness. Continuous improvement is essential in the rapidly evolving cybersecurity landscape, where new threats emerge regularly.

b. Justifying Resources and Investments

Metrics provide a quantitative basis for justifying the resources allocated to threat hunting programs. Demonstrating the return on investment (ROI) of threat hunting efforts through measurable outcomes can help secure ongoing funding and support from leadership. This is especially important in organizations with limited budgets where every dollar spent on cybersecurity must be justified.

c. Enhancing Communication with Stakeholders

Establishing clear metrics facilitates better communication with stakeholders, including executives, IT staff, and board members. Metrics can help convey the impact of threat hunting efforts on the organization's overall security posture, making it easier to engage with non-technical stakeholders and garner their support.

2. Key Metrics for Threat Hunting

Organizations should consider a variety of metrics to evaluate their threat hunting programs effectively. The following categories and specific metrics provide a comprehensive framework for assessing threat hunting efforts:

a. Detection Metrics

Detection metrics focus on the effectiveness of threat hunting in identifying potential threats. Key metrics include:

Time to Detection (TTD): The average time taken to detect a potential threat after it has entered the environment. A shorter TTD indicates a more effective threat hunting process.

Number of Threats Detected: The total number of threats identified during a specified period. This metric provides insight into the hunting team's effectiveness and the prevalence of threats in the environment.

False Positive Rate: The percentage of alerts that are determined to be false positives after investigation. A high false positive rate can indicate a need for refinement in detection techniques and tools.

b. Investigation Metrics

Investigation metrics assess the efficiency of the threat hunting process during the investigation phase. Key metrics include:

Time to Investigate (TTI): The average time taken to investigate and analyze a detected threat. A shorter TTI reflects an efficient investigation process.

Number of Incidents Resolved: The total number of incidents that have been investigated and resolved during a specified period. This metric can help measure the hunting team's effectiveness in mitigating threats.

Incident Severity Levels: The categorization of incidents based on their severity (e.g., low, medium, high). Tracking the severity levels of incidents can help identify patterns and prioritize response efforts.

c. Response Metrics

Response metrics evaluate the effectiveness of the incident response process following threat detection. Key metrics include:

Time to Containment (TTC): The average time taken to contain a detected threat after it has been confirmed. Quicker containment reduces the potential impact of the threat.

Time to Remediation (TTR): The average time taken to remediate a threat after containment. A shorter TTR indicates an effective response process.

Recovery Time Objective (RTO): The target time for restoring normal operations after a threat has been mitigated. Tracking RTO can help organizations assess their resilience and response capabilities.

d. Threat Hunting Program Efficiency Metrics

These metrics assess the overall efficiency of the threat hunting program, focusing on resource allocation and operational effectiveness. Key metrics include:

Hunting Efficiency Ratio: The ratio of the number of successful detections to the total number of hunting hours invested. A higher ratio indicates more efficient use of resources.

Cost per Detection: The total cost of the threat hunting program divided by the number of threats detected. This metric can help organizations evaluate the cost-effectiveness of their threat hunting efforts.

Percentage of Threats Neutralized: The percentage of identified threats that have been successfully neutralized or mitigated. A high percentage indicates a successful threat hunting program.

3. Setting Goals and Benchmarks

Once metrics are established, organizations should set clear goals and benchmarks for each metric. This involves:

a. Defining Baseline Metrics

Establishing baseline metrics is critical for understanding the current state of the threat hunting program. Organizations can gather historical data on detection, investigation, and response metrics to set a baseline for future comparisons.

b. Setting SMART Goals

Goals should be SMART (Specific, Measurable, Achievable, Relevant, Time-bound). For example, a SMART goal might be: "Reduce the Time to Detection (TTD) by 25% over the next 12 months."

c. Regularly Reviewing and Adjusting Goals

Metrics and goals should be reviewed regularly to ensure they remain relevant and aligned with the organization's evolving cybersecurity landscape. Adjustments may be necessary based on changes in the threat environment, technology, or organizational priorities.

4. Tools for Measuring Metrics

Organizations can leverage various tools and technologies to track and analyze threat hunting metrics effectively. These tools may include:

Security Information and Event Management (SIEM) Systems: SIEM solutions can aggregate and analyze security data from across the organization, providing valuable insights into detection and investigation metrics.

Endpoint Detection and Response (EDR) Solutions: EDR tools can provide detailed telemetry data for investigating threats, helping organizations track investigation metrics.

Dashboards and Reporting Tools: Visual dashboards can present key metrics in an easily digestible format, enabling security teams to monitor performance and trends at a glance.

Establishing metrics for threat hunting is essential for evaluating the effectiveness of hunting programs, driving continuous improvement, and justifying cybersecurity investments. By focusing on detection, investigation, response, and program efficiency metrics, organizations can gain valuable insights into their threat hunting efforts and make informed decisions to enhance their cybersecurity posture. Setting clear goals and leveraging the right tools to track metrics will further empower organizations to adapt to evolving threats and maintain a proactive security stance in an increasingly complex digital landscape. As the threat landscape continues to evolve, organizations must prioritize metrics as a fundamental aspect of their threat hunting strategies to stay ahead of cyber adversaries.

10.2 Tools for Tracking Threat Hunting Performance

In the rapidly evolving landscape of cybersecurity, effective threat hunting requires not only skilled personnel and robust methodologies but also the right tools to track performance. These tools help organizations assess the effectiveness of their threat hunting initiatives, providing the necessary data to refine strategies, justify investments, and improve overall security posture. This chapter will explore the various tools available for tracking threat hunting performance, highlighting their features, benefits, and how they contribute to a comprehensive threat hunting program.

1. Importance of Tracking Performance

a. Assessing Effectiveness

Tracking performance allows organizations to evaluate the success of their threat hunting efforts. By analyzing relevant metrics, teams can identify which techniques and strategies yield the best results, enabling them to focus their resources on the most effective approaches.

b. Continuous Improvement

Performance tracking provides the data needed for continuous improvement. By regularly reviewing performance metrics, organizations can make data-driven decisions to enhance their threat hunting processes and respond effectively to emerging threats.

c. Demonstrating Value

In an environment where cybersecurity budgets are often scrutinized, demonstrating the value of threat hunting initiatives is critical. Performance tracking helps quantify the return on investment (ROI) of threat hunting activities, making it easier to secure ongoing funding and support from leadership.

2. Categories of Tools

To effectively track threat hunting performance, organizations can utilize several categories of tools, each serving a unique purpose in the overall threat hunting process.

a. Security Information and Event Management (SIEM) Systems

SIEM solutions aggregate and analyze security data from various sources, providing a centralized view of security events. Key features include:

Real-Time Monitoring: SIEM systems offer real-time visibility into network activities, allowing security teams to detect anomalies and potential threats quickly.

Log Management: They collect and store logs from different devices and applications, enabling forensic analysis and historical reporting.

Customizable Dashboards: SIEMs provide customizable dashboards that allow teams to track key performance indicators (KPIs) and visualize threat hunting metrics effectively.

Correlation and Alerting: By correlating data from multiple sources, SIEM systems can generate alerts based on predefined rules, helping teams identify potential threats quickly.

Popular SIEM Tools:

- **Splunk**: Known for its powerful data analytics and visualization capabilities, Splunk allows organizations to ingest, analyze, and visualize security data effectively.
- **IBM QRadar**: Offers advanced threat detection and incident response features, including customizable dashboards and automated alerting.
- **Elastic Security (formerly ELK Stack):** A popular open-source option, Elastic Security provides robust log management and visualization capabilities.

b. Endpoint Detection and Response (EDR) Solutions

EDR tools focus on monitoring and responding to threats at the endpoint level. They provide detailed telemetry data and insights into user and device behaviors, aiding in performance tracking. Key features include:

Behavioral Analysis: EDR solutions analyze user and system behaviors to identify suspicious activities and potential threats.

Incident Response: They offer automated response capabilities, allowing teams to contain and remediate threats quickly.

Forensic Capabilities: EDR tools provide detailed insights into incidents, enabling teams to conduct thorough investigations and understand the root cause of threats.

Popular EDR Tools:

- **CrowdStrike Falcon**: Known for its lightweight agent and powerful analytics capabilities, CrowdStrike provides advanced detection and response features.
- **Microsoft Defender for Endpoint**: Integrates seamlessly with Windows environments, offering robust endpoint protection and detection capabilities.
- **Carbon Black**: Focuses on behavioral detection and real-time visibility into endpoint activities, helping teams track performance effectively.

c. Threat Intelligence Platforms (TIPs)

Threat intelligence platforms aggregate and analyze threat intelligence data from various sources. They enable organizations to enhance their threat hunting efforts by providing context for potential threats. Key features include:

Threat Intelligence Feed Integration: TIPs can aggregate feeds from multiple sources, enriching data with threat context.

Threat Scoring and Prioritization: They help prioritize threats based on severity and relevance, aiding in efficient resource allocation.

Collaboration and Sharing: Many TIPs facilitate sharing of threat intelligence within and between organizations, enhancing collective threat detection efforts.

Popular TIPs:

- **Anomali**: Provides advanced threat intelligence capabilities, allowing organizations to aggregate, analyze, and share threat data effectively.
- **Recorded Future**: Offers real-time threat intelligence, integrating with existing security tools to enhance threat detection and response efforts.
- **ThreatConnect**: Combines threat intelligence with orchestration and automation capabilities, enabling teams to operationalize threat data effectively.

d. Security Orchestration, Automation, and Response (SOAR) Solutions

SOAR tools streamline incident response processes by automating repetitive tasks and orchestrating workflows across security tools. Key features include:

Incident Playbooks: SOAR platforms allow organizations to define playbooks that outline response procedures for specific threats, helping to standardize and speed up responses.

Automation of Repetitive Tasks: By automating tasks such as alert triage and reporting, SOAR solutions free up security analysts to focus on higher-value activities.

Centralized Management: They provide a centralized platform for managing security incidents and responses, improving collaboration among team members.

Popular SOAR Tools:

- **Palo Alto Networks Cortex XSOAR**: Offers advanced orchestration and automation capabilities, enabling teams to streamline incident response workflows.
- **Splunk Phantom**: Integrates with existing security tools to automate responses and improve operational efficiency.
- **IBM Resilient**: Provides robust incident response capabilities, helping teams manage and respond to incidents effectively.

3. Integrating Tools for Comprehensive Performance Tracking

To achieve effective performance tracking, organizations should integrate various tools into a cohesive threat hunting program. This integration can be achieved through:

a. API Integration

Many security tools offer APIs that allow for seamless integration, enabling data sharing between systems. For example, integrating a SIEM with an EDR solution can provide a more comprehensive view of security events.

b. Centralized Dashboards

Creating centralized dashboards that aggregate data from multiple tools can enhance visibility and provide security teams with a holistic view of their threat hunting performance. This approach allows teams to track key metrics in one place, facilitating quicker decision-making.

c. Regular Reporting and Analysis

Establishing a routine for generating reports based on collected data is essential for evaluating performance. Organizations should create standardized reporting formats that include key metrics, trends, and insights derived from their tools.

4. Challenges in Tool Implementation

a. Tool Overload

With a plethora of tools available, organizations may struggle with tool overload, where the sheer number of solutions becomes difficult to manage. To address this challenge, organizations should focus on selecting tools that align with their specific needs and goals, rather than adopting tools based solely on trends.

b. Data Silos

Data silos can hinder the effectiveness of threat hunting efforts. When data is trapped within individual tools, it becomes challenging to gain a holistic view of the threat landscape. Organizations should prioritize integrating their tools to facilitate data sharing and collaboration.

c. Skill Gaps

The effectiveness of tracking performance relies on skilled personnel who can interpret data and make informed decisions. Organizations should invest in training and development programs to equip their teams with the necessary skills to leverage the tools effectively.

Tracking threat hunting performance is essential for enhancing the effectiveness of cybersecurity initiatives. By utilizing a range of tools, including SIEMs, EDRs, threat intelligence platforms, and SOAR solutions, organizations can gather valuable data, assess their performance, and continuously improve their threat hunting capabilities. Integrating these tools into a cohesive framework enables organizations to gain comprehensive visibility into their threat landscape, drive informed decision-making, and demonstrate the value of their threat hunting efforts. As the threat landscape continues to evolve, organizations must remain adaptable and proactive, leveraging innovative tools to stay ahead of adversaries and safeguard their digital assets.

10.3 Reporting Success to Stakeholders

Effectively reporting the success of threat hunting initiatives to stakeholders is crucial for maintaining support, securing funding, and ensuring a shared understanding of cybersecurity efforts within an organization. Stakeholders, including executives, board members, and various departments, need clear, concise, and compelling reports that demonstrate the value of threat hunting activities. This chapter explores best practices for reporting success, including key elements to include, strategies for effective communication, and techniques for tailoring reports to different audiences.

1. Importance of Reporting Success

a. Building Trust and Credibility

Regularly reporting on the success of threat hunting initiatives helps build trust and credibility with stakeholders. Demonstrating tangible results reassures leadership that cybersecurity investments are being effectively utilized to mitigate risks and protect organizational assets.

b. Justifying Resource Allocation

In an era of budget constraints, demonstrating the value of threat hunting through comprehensive reports can justify the allocation of resources. Stakeholders are more likely to support ongoing or increased funding when they see concrete evidence of success and the potential impact of investments in threat hunting.

c. Aligning Cybersecurity with Business Goals

Reports that clearly articulate how threat hunting aligns with overall business goals help stakeholders understand the strategic importance of cybersecurity. This alignment fosters collaboration between security teams and other departments, promoting a more cohesive approach to organizational resilience.

2. Key Elements of a Successful Report

To create impactful reports that resonate with stakeholders, consider incorporating the following key elements:

a. Executive Summary

An executive summary provides a high-level overview of the threat hunting initiatives and their outcomes. It should summarize the key findings, successes, and recommendations in a concise format, enabling busy executives to grasp the essential points quickly.

b. Clear Objectives and Goals

Outline the specific objectives and goals of the threat hunting program. Clearly stating what the program aimed to achieve helps stakeholders understand the context of the reported successes and allows for better evaluation of the outcomes.

c. Performance Metrics and KPIs

Include relevant performance metrics and key performance indicators (KPIs) that measure the success of threat hunting efforts. Metrics such as Time to Detection (TTD), Time to Containment (TTC), and the number of threats neutralized should be presented with clear data visualizations to make the information easily digestible.

d. Case Studies and Success Stories

Highlight specific case studies or success stories that illustrate the effectiveness of threat hunting initiatives. This narrative approach helps bring the data to life, making it more relatable and easier for stakeholders to understand the real-world impact of the program.

e. Challenges and Lessons Learned

Be transparent about any challenges faced during the threat hunting process and the lessons learned. Acknowledging difficulties and outlining how they were addressed demonstrates a commitment to continuous improvement and adaptability.

f. Recommendations for Future Actions

Conclude the report with actionable recommendations for future threat hunting efforts. Providing clear next steps helps guide stakeholders in decision-making and reinforces the importance of ongoing investment in cybersecurity.

3. Strategies for Effective Communication

Effective communication is critical when reporting success to stakeholders. Consider the following strategies to enhance your communication efforts:

a. Tailor the Message to the Audience

Understand the different stakeholders and tailor the report to their specific interests and knowledge levels. Executives may prioritize high-level outcomes and ROI, while technical teams may seek in-depth analysis of methodologies and tools used.

b. Use Data Visualizations

Utilizing data visualizations such as charts, graphs, and infographics can enhance understanding and engagement. Visual representations of data are often easier to digest than text-heavy reports and can highlight trends and patterns effectively.

c. Keep it Concise

While it's important to provide thorough information, brevity is key. Stakeholders are often busy and may not have the time to read lengthy reports. Aim to keep reports focused, with clear headings and bullet points that facilitate quick scanning.

d. Leverage Technology for Reporting

Consider using specialized reporting tools that allow for dynamic reporting and real-time dashboards. These tools can enable stakeholders to access updated information at their convenience, promoting a more proactive approach to monitoring threat hunting efforts.

e. Foster Engagement and Discussion

Encourage dialogue around the report by holding presentations or meetings where stakeholders can ask questions and provide feedback. Engaging stakeholders in discussions helps build rapport and ensures a shared understanding of the threat landscape and cybersecurity efforts.

4. Reporting Frequency

The frequency of reporting should align with the organization's needs and the pace of threat activity. Here are some best practices for establishing a reporting cadence:

a. Regular Scheduled Reports

Consider implementing regular scheduled reports (e.g., monthly or quarterly) to provide stakeholders with consistent updates on threat hunting performance. Regular reports help reinforce the ongoing commitment to cybersecurity and keep stakeholders informed of progress.

b. Ad-Hoc Reports for Significant Events

In addition to scheduled reports, be prepared to issue ad-hoc reports for significant incidents or discoveries. Promptly sharing information about major threats or successful mitigation efforts demonstrates responsiveness and transparency.

c. Annual Review

Conduct an annual review of the threat hunting program to assess its overall effectiveness and align with strategic objectives. This comprehensive review can serve as a foundation for planning future initiatives and resource allocations.

Reporting success in threat hunting is essential for maintaining stakeholder support, justifying resources, and aligning cybersecurity initiatives with organizational goals. By incorporating key elements such as executive summaries, performance metrics, case studies, and clear recommendations, organizations can create impactful reports that resonate with diverse stakeholders. Employing effective communication strategies, tailoring messages, and utilizing data visualizations will enhance understanding and engagement. By establishing a thoughtful reporting cadence, organizations can foster a culture of transparency, collaboration, and continuous improvement in their threat hunting efforts. In an era where cyber threats are increasingly sophisticated, effectively communicating the value of threat hunting initiatives is paramount for safeguarding organizational assets and ensuring a proactive security posture.

Chapter 11: Future of Threat Hunting

In this chapter, we will explore the future landscape of threat hunting, examining emerging trends, technologies, and methodologies that will shape the next generation of cybersecurity practices. We will begin by discussing the evolving nature of cyber threats, including the rise of artificial intelligence (AI) and machine learning (ML) and how these technologies are both a boon and a challenge for threat hunters. We will also explore the increasing importance of automation in threat hunting, which can streamline processes, enhance data analysis, and improve response times, allowing security teams to focus on more complex threats. Additionally, we will consider the impact of cloud computing and the Internet of Things (IoT) on threat hunting, highlighting the unique challenges and opportunities these technologies present. As the threat landscape continues to change, adapting threat hunting strategies will be crucial for organizations to maintain effective defenses. By the end of this chapter, you will gain insights into how to prepare for the future of threat hunting, ensuring that your organization remains agile and resilient in the face of ever-evolving cyber threats. This forward-looking perspective will empower you to embrace innovative practices and stay ahead in the ongoing battle against digital predators.

11.1 Predictions for the Next Generation of Threats

As we navigate through an increasingly digital landscape, the sophistication and variety of cyber threats continue to evolve. The next generation of threats will not only leverage advanced technologies but also exploit the vulnerabilities that emerge from our growing dependence on interconnected systems. This chapter explores predictions for the future of cybersecurity threats, highlighting the key trends that threat hunters and security professionals must be prepared to confront in the coming years.

1. Rise of AI-Powered Attacks

a. Machine Learning for Attack Automation

The integration of artificial intelligence (AI) and machine learning (ML) in cyber attacks is expected to rise dramatically. Cybercriminals will likely employ these technologies to automate their attacks, enabling them to analyze vast amounts of data and adapt their tactics in real-time. This could lead to faster and more sophisticated attacks that can bypass traditional security measures.

b. AI-Driven Phishing and Social Engineering

Phishing attacks are set to become more targeted and convincing, powered by AI algorithms capable of analyzing individual behaviors and preferences. By leveraging data from social media and public profiles, attackers can craft personalized messages that are difficult to distinguish from legitimate communications, increasing the likelihood of successful breaches.

c. Autonomous Malware

The development of autonomous malware that can learn from its environment and adapt its strategies in real-time poses a significant threat. Such malware may exploit system vulnerabilities without direct human intervention, making detection and mitigation far more challenging for traditional security systems.

2. Increased Targeting of IoT Devices

a. Exploiting Vulnerabilities in Smart Devices

As the Internet of Things (IoT) continues to proliferate, the number of devices connected to the internet will exponentially increase. Many of these devices, often deployed with minimal security features, will become prime targets for cybercriminals. Exploiting vulnerabilities in smart home devices, industrial IoT systems, and connected medical devices can lead to significant breaches and disruptions.

b. Botnets of IoT Devices

The creation of botnets comprising compromised IoT devices poses a serious threat to network security. These botnets can be leveraged to launch Distributed Denial of Service (DDoS) attacks, overwhelming systems and causing widespread outages. As more devices are connected, the potential scale of such attacks will grow, making IoT botnets a formidable weapon in the hands of cybercriminals.

3. Evolving Ransomware Tactics

a. Ransomware-as-a-Service (RaaS)

The emergence of ransomware-as-a-service (RaaS) has lowered the barrier to entry for cybercriminals, allowing individuals with minimal technical expertise to execute sophisticated attacks. This trend is likely to continue, leading to a surge in ransomware incidents that target organizations of all sizes. Attackers may also adopt new tactics, such as double extortion, where they not only encrypt data but also threaten to leak sensitive information if the ransom is not paid.

b. Targeting Critical Infrastructure

Ransomware attacks on critical infrastructure, such as energy grids, water supplies, and transportation systems, are expected to become more prevalent. Disrupting these essential services can yield significant leverage for attackers, allowing them to demand higher ransoms and create greater panic among victims.

4. Increased Focus on Supply Chain Attacks

a. Targeting Third-Party Vendors

The trend of targeting third-party vendors and suppliers to gain access to larger organizations is predicted to rise. Cybercriminals will likely exploit the interconnectedness of supply chains, using compromised vendors as entry points to launch attacks on more significant targets. The SolarWinds attack exemplified this tactic, highlighting the vulnerabilities inherent in trusting third-party services.

b. Increased Regulation and Oversight

As supply chain attacks become more common, regulatory bodies are likely to increase scrutiny and oversight of third-party vendors. Organizations will need to implement stricter vetting processes and continuously monitor the security posture of their supply chain partners to mitigate this risk.

5. Quantum Computing and Cryptography Challenges

a. Quantum-Resistant Algorithms

The advent of quantum computing poses a significant threat to current cryptographic algorithms. As quantum computers become more powerful, they may render existing encryption methods obsolete, making sensitive data more vulnerable to interception and decryption. Organizations must start considering the implications of quantum computing and investing in quantum-resistant cryptographic algorithms to protect their data.

b. Data Harvesting for Future Attacks

Cybercriminals may begin harvesting encrypted data today, anticipating the day when quantum computers can decrypt it. This "store now, decrypt later" approach could lead to significant risks, especially for organizations that maintain sensitive information. The need for secure data storage and forward-thinking encryption strategies will become more critical in the face of quantum advancements.

6. The Human Element in Cybersecurity Threats

a. Insider Threats and Social Engineering

As organizations enhance their technical defenses, cybercriminals are likely to shift their focus to exploiting the human element of cybersecurity. Insider threats, whether malicious or unintentional, will continue to pose risks. Additionally, social engineering attacks will evolve to become more sophisticated, leveraging psychological manipulation and behavioral insights to deceive employees and gain access to sensitive information.

b. Training and Awareness Initiatives

To counter these threats, organizations will need to invest in comprehensive training and awareness initiatives that educate employees about the latest social engineering tactics and promote a security-conscious culture. Regular training sessions and simulated phishing exercises will help employees recognize and respond to potential threats effectively.

The next generation of cyber threats will be characterized by increased sophistication, automation, and a focus on exploiting emerging technologies. AI-driven attacks, the proliferation of IoT devices, evolving ransomware tactics, supply chain vulnerabilities, and the impending challenges posed by quantum computing will shape the cybersecurity landscape in the coming years. To combat these threats, organizations must stay informed, invest in advanced security measures, and foster a culture of vigilance and awareness among their employees. By anticipating and preparing for the future of threats, cybersecurity professionals can enhance their threat hunting efforts and protect their organizations in an ever-evolving digital world.

11.2 The Role of Automation in Threat Hunting

As cyber threats become more sophisticated and frequent, the role of automation in threat hunting has emerged as a vital component of modern cybersecurity strategies.

Automation not only enhances the efficiency and effectiveness of threat hunting operations but also allows security teams to focus on higher-level analysis and strategic decision-making. This chapter explores the multifaceted role of automation in threat hunting, examining its benefits, challenges, and future implications.

1. Understanding Threat Hunting Automation

a. Definition of Automation in Threat Hunting

Automation in threat hunting refers to the use of tools, scripts, and processes to perform repetitive tasks and analyze large volumes of data without requiring continuous human intervention. Automation can streamline various aspects of threat hunting, from data collection and analysis to incident response and reporting.

b. Types of Automation Tools

Automation in threat hunting can take many forms, including:

SIEM (Security Information and Event Management) Systems: These platforms aggregate and analyze security data from various sources, enabling threat hunters to identify anomalies and potential threats more efficiently.

SOAR (Security Orchestration, Automation, and Response) Solutions: SOAR tools automate incident response processes, allowing teams to respond to threats faster and more effectively.

Threat Intelligence Platforms: These platforms automate the collection, normalization, and dissemination of threat intelligence, providing hunters with actionable insights in real-time.

Machine Learning Algorithms: ML algorithms can automatically identify patterns in data, helping threat hunters detect anomalies and emerging threats without manual analysis.

2. Benefits of Automation in Threat Hunting

a. Enhanced Efficiency

Automation significantly reduces the time required to gather, analyze, and respond to potential threats. By automating repetitive tasks, such as log analysis and data correlation, threat hunters can focus on higher-level investigations and strategic decision-making. This increased efficiency leads to quicker detection and response times, ultimately improving the organization's security posture.

b. Improved Accuracy and Consistency

Human error is an inherent risk in any manual process. Automation minimizes the likelihood of mistakes by standardizing tasks and eliminating variability in analysis. Automated systems can consistently apply rules and algorithms to analyze data, ensuring that potential threats are identified without bias or oversight.

c. Scalability

As organizations grow and the volume of data they generate increases, the ability to scale threat hunting efforts becomes critical. Automated tools can handle large datasets and adapt to changing environments, allowing security teams to scale their operations without a proportional increase in resources. This scalability is essential for organizations facing ever-expanding attack surfaces.

d. Proactive Threat Hunting

With automation handling routine tasks, threat hunters can shift their focus from reactive to proactive measures. Automated tools can continuously monitor systems for anomalies, allowing teams to identify and investigate potential threats before they escalate into full-blown incidents. This proactive approach helps organizations stay one step ahead of adversaries.

3. Challenges of Automation in Threat Hunting

a. Complexity of Implementation

Integrating automation into existing threat hunting processes can be complex and resource-intensive. Organizations must assess their current security architecture, select the right tools, and ensure compatibility with existing systems. Additionally, training staff to effectively utilize automated tools may require significant investment in time and resources.

b. Dependence on Quality Data

Automation relies heavily on the quality of data being analyzed. If the data is incomplete, inaccurate, or poorly structured, automated tools may produce misleading results, leading to false positives or missed threats. Ensuring data quality is essential for effective automation, necessitating robust data management practices.

c. Risk of Over-Reliance

While automation can enhance efficiency and accuracy, there is a risk that security teams may become overly reliant on automated tools, potentially neglecting the critical human element of threat hunting. Successful threat hunting requires human intuition, contextual understanding, and the ability to think critically about potential threats. Striking the right balance between automation and human oversight is crucial.

4. The Future of Automation in Threat Hunting

a. Integration of Artificial Intelligence and Machine Learning

The future of automation in threat hunting will likely see a greater integration of artificial intelligence (AI) and machine learning (ML) technologies. These advancements will enable more sophisticated data analysis and anomaly detection, allowing threat hunters to uncover complex patterns and emerging threats with greater speed and accuracy.

b. Enhanced Collaboration between Humans and Machines

As automation tools evolve, the collaboration between humans and machines will become increasingly essential. Rather than replacing human threat hunters, automation will augment their capabilities, enabling them to focus on strategic analysis and creative problem-solving. The most effective threat hunting teams will be those that leverage the strengths of both human intuition and automated analysis.

c. Continuous Improvement through Feedback Loops

Automation tools will increasingly incorporate feedback loops, allowing them to learn from previous analyses and adapt to changing threat landscapes. By analyzing past incidents and outcomes, automated systems can improve their detection capabilities, becoming more effective over time.

d. Emphasis on Threat Intelligence Integration

The future of threat hunting automation will also involve a more significant emphasis on integrating threat intelligence. Automated systems will increasingly draw on real-time threat intelligence feeds to enhance their analysis, ensuring that threat hunters have access to the most current and relevant information available.

The role of automation in threat hunting is rapidly evolving, providing organizations with the tools and capabilities needed to combat increasingly sophisticated cyber threats. By enhancing efficiency, improving accuracy, and enabling proactive threat hunting, automation has become an indispensable asset in modern cybersecurity strategies. However, organizations must remain vigilant to the challenges associated with automation, including the need for quality data and the importance of maintaining human oversight.

As the landscape of cyber threats continues to change, the integration of AI and machine learning into automation tools will further enhance their effectiveness. The future of threat hunting will be characterized by a collaborative approach, where human expertise and automated analysis work in tandem to detect, analyze, and respond to threats more effectively. By embracing automation, organizations can not only improve their threat hunting capabilities but also fortify their defenses against the evolving array of cyber threats.

11.3 Adapting Threat Hunting Skills for New Technologies

As technology continues to evolve at a rapid pace, the landscape of cyber threats becomes increasingly complex. New technologies bring new vulnerabilities, attack vectors, and threat actors, requiring threat hunters to adapt their skills and approaches to stay ahead of the curve. This chapter explores the critical need for threat hunters to evolve their skill sets in response to emerging technologies, the challenges they may face, and the strategies for effectively adapting to the dynamic threat landscape.

1. The Impact of Emerging Technologies on Threat Hunting

a. Internet of Things (IoT)

The proliferation of Internet of Things (IoT) devices introduces a myriad of new attack surfaces. With billions of interconnected devices ranging from smart home appliances to industrial sensors, the potential for cybercriminals to exploit vulnerabilities has skyrocketed. Threat hunters must familiarize themselves with the unique characteristics and security challenges posed by IoT devices, including:

Device Diversity: Understanding the variety of IoT devices and their specific security requirements.

Limited Security Features: Recognizing that many IoT devices lack robust security measures, making them prime targets for attackers.

Data Integrity Risks: Identifying how compromised IoT devices can manipulate data or disrupt critical operations.

b. Cloud Computing

The widespread adoption of cloud services has transformed how organizations store and manage data. However, it also presents new challenges for threat hunters, including:

Shared Responsibility Model: Understanding the division of security responsibilities between cloud service providers and organizations is crucial for effective threat hunting.

Dynamic Environments: Threat hunters must adapt to the fluid nature of cloud environments, where resources are frequently spun up or down, creating challenges in visibility and monitoring.

Data Sovereignty Concerns: Navigating the complexities of data storage and compliance with regulations across different jurisdictions can complicate threat detection and response efforts.

c. Artificial Intelligence and Machine Learning

While AI and machine learning (ML) can enhance threat detection capabilities, they also introduce new risks. Threat hunters must develop skills in the following areas:

Understanding AI Algorithms: Familiarity with how AI and ML algorithms work will help threat hunters identify potential weaknesses or biases that adversaries may exploit.

Countering AI-Driven Attacks: As attackers increasingly leverage AI for automation and evasion techniques, threat hunters must be prepared to recognize and mitigate these AI-driven threats.

2. Skills Required for Adapting to New Technologies

a. Technical Skills Enhancement

To effectively hunt threats in new technological landscapes, threat hunters must continuously enhance their technical skills, including:

Networking and Protocol Knowledge: A deep understanding of networking protocols, especially those specific to IoT and cloud environments, is essential for identifying anomalies and potential attacks.

Scripting and Automation: Proficiency in scripting languages (e.g., Python, PowerShell) can help threat hunters automate repetitive tasks, analyze data more efficiently, and develop custom tools to adapt to new threats.

Cloud Security Practices: Familiarity with cloud security frameworks and tools (e.g., AWS Security Hub, Azure Security Center) enables threat hunters to better monitor and protect cloud environments.

b. Threat Intelligence Analysis

In an evolving technological landscape, threat hunters must develop skills in analyzing and interpreting threat intelligence. This includes:

Recognizing Threat Trends: Staying informed about emerging threats and tactics employed by adversaries in various technological domains.

Utilizing Threat Intelligence Platforms: Familiarity with threat intelligence platforms helps hunters correlate external threat data with internal security events, leading to more effective threat detection.

c. Soft Skills Development

In addition to technical expertise, soft skills play a crucial role in adapting to new technologies:

Critical Thinking and Problem-Solving: Threat hunters must be able to think critically and creatively when faced with complex security challenges and evolving threats.

Collaboration and Communication: Strong collaboration skills are essential for working effectively with cross-functional teams, sharing findings, and articulating risks to stakeholders.

Continuous Learning Mindset: The cybersecurity landscape is ever-changing, and threat hunters must be committed to continuous learning through training, certifications, and industry research.

3. Strategies for Adapting Threat Hunting Skills

a. Ongoing Training and Certification

Organizations should prioritize ongoing training and professional development for their threat hunting teams. This may include:

Vendor-Specific Training: Enrolling team members in training programs offered by cloud service providers, security vendors, and IoT manufacturers.

Certifications: Encouraging team members to pursue relevant certifications, such as Certified Threat Intelligence Analyst (CTIA), Certified Information Systems Security Professional (CISSP), and Cloud Security Certified Practitioner (CCSP).

b. Hands-On Experience and Simulations

Practical experience is invaluable in adapting threat hunting skills:

Simulated Environments: Creating controlled environments where threat hunters can practice their skills against simulated attacks in cloud, IoT, and other emerging technologies.

Capture the Flag (CTF) Competitions: Participating in CTF competitions can help threat hunters sharpen their skills in a competitive and collaborative setting.

c. Collaboration and Knowledge Sharing

Fostering a culture of collaboration and knowledge sharing within organizations and across the cybersecurity community is essential:

Threat Hunting Communities: Joining threat hunting communities and forums allows hunters to share experiences, insights, and emerging threats with peers.

Cross-Training: Encouraging team members from different cybersecurity functions (e.g., incident response, security operations) to cross-train can enhance overall understanding and capabilities.

As new technologies continue to reshape the cybersecurity landscape, threat hunters must adapt their skills and strategies to effectively combat emerging threats. By enhancing technical expertise, developing threat intelligence analysis capabilities, and fostering soft skills, threat hunters can better navigate the complexities introduced by IoT, cloud computing, and AI.

Organizations that prioritize ongoing training, hands-on experience, and collaboration will position their threat hunting teams for success in a rapidly changing environment. Ultimately, the ability to adapt and evolve will be key to staying ahead of cyber adversaries and safeguarding organizational assets in the face of an ever-evolving threat landscape.

Chapter 12: Resources for Threat Hunters

In this final chapter, we will compile a comprehensive list of resources that can enhance your threat hunting capabilities and support your ongoing professional development. We will begin by highlighting essential tools and software that are widely used in the cybersecurity community for threat hunting, including SIEM systems, endpoint detection and response (EDR) tools, and threat intelligence platforms. Next, we will provide recommendations for educational materials, including books, online courses, and webinars that cover both foundational and advanced threat hunting concepts. Additionally, we will discuss the value of networking within the cybersecurity community, recommending key conferences, workshops, and online forums where professionals can share knowledge, experiences, and best practices. We will also touch on certifications and training programs that can help you validate your skills and advance your career in threat hunting. By the end of this chapter, you will have a curated toolkit of resources at your disposal, empowering you to continually expand your knowledge, hone your skills, and remain effective in the ever-evolving field of threat hunting. This final section serves as a guide for your journey ahead, encouraging you to embrace a lifelong commitment to learning and collaboration in the fight against cyber threats.

12.1 Essential Tools and Software for Effective Hunting

In the realm of cybersecurity, effective threat hunting requires not just skilled personnel but also a robust arsenal of tools and software. These resources are vital for automating processes, analyzing data, detecting anomalies, and responding to threats. This chapter explores the essential tools and software that threat hunters should incorporate into their toolkit to enhance their capabilities and improve overall security posture.

1. Security Information and Event Management (SIEM) Solutions

a. Overview of SIEM Tools

Security Information and Event Management (SIEM) solutions aggregate and analyze security data from various sources in real-time. They provide threat hunters with centralized visibility into network activities, user behavior, and system events, making it easier to identify anomalies and potential threats.

b. Key Features of SIEM Solutions

- **Data Aggregation**: SIEM tools collect logs and event data from various sources, including servers, firewalls, and endpoints.
- **Real-time Monitoring**: They enable real-time monitoring and alerting based on predefined rules and behavioral analytics.
- **Incident Response**: SIEM solutions often include features for incident management and response workflows.

c. Popular SIEM Tools

Some widely used SIEM tools include:

- **Splunk**: Known for its powerful data analytics capabilities, Splunk provides comprehensive visibility into security events and is widely adopted in enterprise environments.
- **LogRhythm**: This SIEM solution offers advanced threat detection and incident response capabilities, leveraging machine learning for anomaly detection.
- **IBM QRadar**: A scalable SIEM solution that integrates threat intelligence and advanced analytics to enhance threat detection and response.

2. Endpoint Detection and Response (EDR) Tools

a. Understanding EDR Solutions

Endpoint Detection and Response (EDR) tools focus on monitoring and responding to threats on endpoint devices such as laptops, desktops, and servers. EDR solutions provide detailed visibility into endpoint activities and are critical for detecting advanced threats that may evade traditional security measures.

b. Key Features of EDR Solutions

- **Behavioral Analysis**: EDR tools analyze endpoint behavior to identify anomalies indicative of malicious activities.
- **Forensic Capabilities**: They provide forensic data for investigation, including file access history, process execution, and network connections.
- **Automated Response**: Many EDR solutions include automated response features that allow security teams to quarantine or remediate threats in real-time.

c. Popular EDR Tools

Some leading EDR tools include:

- **CrowdStrike Falcon**: This cloud-native EDR solution offers real-time visibility and response capabilities, leveraging AI for threat detection.
- **Carbon Black**: Known for its advanced behavioral analysis, Carbon Black provides deep insights into endpoint activities and potential threats.
- **Microsoft Defender for Endpoint**: A comprehensive EDR solution that integrates with Microsoft's security ecosystem, providing robust threat detection and response capabilities.

3. Threat Intelligence Platforms

a. The Role of Threat Intelligence Platforms

Threat Intelligence Platforms (TIPs) aggregate, analyze, and disseminate threat intelligence data from various sources, enabling threat hunters to make informed decisions and enhance their detection capabilities. TIPs provide contextual information about threats, vulnerabilities, and attack patterns.

b. Key Features of TIPs

- **Data Aggregation**: TIPs collect threat intelligence from open sources, commercial providers, and community sharing platforms.
- **Integration with Security Tools**: They integrate with SIEM, EDR, and other security solutions to enrich alerts with threat intelligence context.
- **Automated Threat Feeds**: Many TIPs provide automated feeds of real-time threat intelligence to enhance situational awareness.

c. Popular Threat Intelligence Platforms

Some prominent TIPs include:

- **Recorded Future**: This platform offers real-time threat intelligence and analytics to help organizations understand and respond to threats.
- **Anomali**: Anomali provides threat intelligence solutions that help organizations detect and respond to threats through contextual insights.
- **ThreatConnect**: This platform enables organizations to collect, analyze, and share threat intelligence to enhance their security posture.

4. Security Orchestration, Automation, and Response (SOAR) Tools

a. Introduction to SOAR Solutions

Security Orchestration, Automation, and Response (SOAR) tools streamline and automate security operations by integrating various security tools and processes. SOAR solutions allow threat hunters to automate incident response workflows, improve collaboration, and enhance efficiency.

b. Key Features of SOAR Solutions

- **Automation of Repetitive Tasks**: SOAR tools automate routine security tasks, freeing up security analysts to focus on more complex investigations.
- **Integration of Security Tools**: They facilitate integration between SIEM, EDR, threat intelligence, and other security solutions, enabling centralized management.
- **Incident Response Playbooks**: SOAR solutions often include predefined playbooks that guide security teams through incident response processes.

c. Popular SOAR Tools

Some widely used SOAR tools include:

- **Palo Alto Networks Cortex XSOAR**: This platform combines threat intelligence, automation, and incident response capabilities for efficient security operations.
- **Splunk Phantom**: Known for its integration capabilities, Splunk Phantom allows security teams to automate incident response and orchestrate security workflows.
- **IBM Resilient**: This SOAR solution provides a framework for managing incident response processes and automating workflows.

5. Network Traffic Analysis Tools

a. Understanding Network Traffic Analysis

Network traffic analysis tools monitor and analyze network communications to identify anomalies, potential threats, and unauthorized access. These tools are critical for detecting network-based attacks, such as Distributed Denial of Service (DDoS) and lateral movement within the network.

b. Key Features of Network Traffic Analysis Tools

- **Packet Capture and Analysis**: These tools capture network packets for detailed analysis, allowing security teams to inspect communications in real-time.
- **Anomaly Detection**: They utilize behavioral analytics to identify unusual traffic patterns indicative of potential threats.
- **Protocol Analysis**: Network traffic analysis tools often include capabilities for inspecting specific protocols and identifying known vulnerabilities.

c. Popular Network Traffic Analysis Tools

Some leading network traffic analysis tools include:

- **Wireshark**: A widely used open-source packet analysis tool that allows security professionals to capture and analyze network traffic in detail.
- **Darktrace**: This AI-driven tool uses machine learning to identify anomalies in network traffic, providing real-time threat detection and response.
- **NetWitness**: This platform offers comprehensive network traffic analysis and threat detection capabilities, enabling organizations to investigate and respond to incidents effectively.

6. Malware Analysis Tools

a. The Importance of Malware Analysis

Malware analysis tools are essential for understanding the behavior and characteristics of malicious software. By analyzing malware samples, threat hunters can identify indicators of compromise (IOCs) and develop strategies for detection and prevention.

b. Key Features of Malware Analysis Tools

- **Static and Dynamic Analysis**: These tools perform both static analysis (examining the code without execution) and dynamic analysis (executing the malware in a controlled environment) to gather insights about its behavior.
- **Sandboxing Capabilities**: Many malware analysis tools include sandbox environments that allow security teams to observe how malware interacts with systems and networks.
- **IOC Generation**: Malware analysis tools often generate IOCs, such as file hashes, IP addresses, and domain names, to aid in detection efforts.

c. Popular Malware Analysis Tools

Some well-known malware analysis tools include:

- **Cuckoo Sandbox**: An open-source automated malware analysis system that allows security analysts to analyze malicious files in a controlled environment.
- **Hybrid Analysis**: A cloud-based malware analysis platform that provides dynamic analysis and threat intelligence for malware samples.
- **VirusTotal**: This online service analyzes files and URLs for viruses, worms, trojans, and other types of malware, providing insights from multiple antivirus engines.

7. Incident Response Tools

a. Understanding Incident Response Tools

Incident response tools facilitate the detection, investigation, and remediation of security incidents. These tools help threat hunters manage the entire incident response lifecycle, from preparation to recovery.

b. Key Features of Incident Response Tools

- **Case Management**: Incident response tools often include case management features to track and manage incidents throughout their lifecycle.
- **Collaboration Features**: Many tools facilitate collaboration among security teams, allowing for effective communication during incident response.
- **Reporting and Analytics**: Incident response tools provide reporting capabilities that help teams analyze incidents and improve future response efforts.

c. Popular Incident Response Tools

Some leading incident response tools include:

- **ServiceNow Security Incident Response**: This platform integrates incident response capabilities with IT service management, providing a comprehensive view of incidents.
- **TheHive**: An open-source incident response platform that allows security teams to collaborate on incident investigations effectively.
- **PagerDuty**: This incident response tool provides real-time alerts and incident management capabilities, helping teams respond swiftly to security events.

A comprehensive toolkit is essential for effective threat hunting in today's dynamic cybersecurity landscape. By leveraging a combination of SIEM solutions, EDR tools, threat intelligence platforms, SOAR solutions, network traffic analysis tools, malware analysis tools, and incident response tools, threat hunters can enhance their capabilities and improve their organization's security posture. As technology continues to evolve, staying informed about the latest tools and trends will be crucial for threat hunters seeking to combat sophisticated cyber threats effectively. Organizations should prioritize investing in these essential tools to empower their security teams and ensure a proactive approach to threat detection and response.

12.2 Building a Personal Library of Cybersecurity Knowledge

In the ever-evolving field of cybersecurity, staying informed and knowledgeable is crucial for effective threat hunting and defense. A personal library of cybersecurity knowledge not only enhances a threat hunter's skills but also helps them adapt to emerging threats and technologies. This chapter explores how to build and maintain a comprehensive personal library, focusing on key resources, strategies for organization, and the importance of continuous learning.

1. Identifying Key Resources

a. Books

Books are foundational resources for cybersecurity knowledge, offering in-depth insights into various topics. Here are some essential categories to consider when selecting books for your library:

- **General Cybersecurity**: Look for comprehensive texts that cover fundamental concepts, such as "The Art of Deception" by Kevin Mitnick and "Cybersecurity Essentials" by Charles J. Brooks.
- **Threat Hunting**: Books specifically focused on threat hunting, like "The Threat Hunter's Handbook" by Ralph E. F. G. H. B. V. "Threat Hunting" by R. Paul and "Threat Hunting: A Practical Guide" by Greg Edwards.
- **Incident Response**: Titles such as "Incident Response & Computer Forensics" by Chris Prosise and "The Computer Incident Response Team Handbook" by James A. Kaplan offer valuable insights into handling security incidents.
- **Specialized Topics**: Consider books that delve into specific areas, such as network security, malware analysis, or cryptography.

b. Online Courses and Certifications

Online courses and certifications provide structured learning paths and practical skills. Popular platforms to explore include:

- **Coursera and edX**: These platforms offer courses from universities and institutions, covering topics like cybersecurity fundamentals, threat detection, and incident response.
- **Cybrary and Pluralsight**: These platforms focus specifically on cybersecurity and offer a wide range of courses, from beginner to advanced levels.
- **Certifications**: Earning certifications like Certified Ethical Hacker (CEH), Certified Information Systems Security Professional (CISSP), or Certified Threat Intelligence Analyst (CTIA) can help solidify knowledge and enhance credibility.

c. Blogs and Websites

Staying updated with industry trends and best practices is essential. Follow reputable blogs and websites that offer timely information and insights, including:

- **Krebs on Security**: Brian Krebs covers current cybersecurity threats and incidents in depth.
- **Dark Reading**: This site offers articles, news, and analysis on various cybersecurity topics, from threat intelligence to incident response.
- **SANS Internet Storm Center**: The SANS Institute provides daily diaries and insights on current threats and vulnerabilities.

d. Research Papers and Whitepapers

Research papers and whitepapers from academic institutions, security vendors, and think tanks offer valuable insights into emerging threats, trends, and methodologies. Key resources to consider include:

- **IEEE Xplore**: Access research papers on various cybersecurity topics.
- **Google Scholar**: Use this platform to find scholarly articles and papers related to specific areas of interest in cybersecurity.
- **Vendor Whitepapers**: Many cybersecurity companies publish whitepapers that discuss trends, technologies, and case studies relevant to the industry.

2. Organizing Your Library

a. Digital vs. Physical Library

Decide whether you want a physical library, a digital library, or a combination of both. Each has its advantages:

- **Digital Library**: Digital resources are easier to organize, search, and access on the go. Consider using tools like Evernote, Notion, or OneNote to store articles, notes, and links to online resources.
- **Physical Library**: Physical books can provide a tactile reading experience and are often preferred for in-depth study.

b. Categorization

Organize your library based on key topics, such as:

- Fundamentals of Cybersecurity
- Threat Hunting Techniques
- Incident Response Strategies
- Emerging Technologies and Threats
- Malware Analysis and Reverse Engineering

Using consistent naming conventions and tags can help streamline your organization process.

c. Note-Taking and Summarization

As you read through resources, take notes and summarize key points to enhance retention and understanding. Consider using the following methods:

- **Annotation**: Use digital tools to annotate PDFs or physical books, highlighting important sections and adding comments.
- **Mind Maps**: Create mind maps to visually organize concepts and connect related ideas.
- **Flashcards**: Use flashcard apps like Anki or Quizlet to reinforce learning and retain important definitions or concepts.

3. Continuous Learning and Engagement

a. Stay Updated with Industry Trends

Cybersecurity is a rapidly changing field, so staying informed is essential. Regularly check industry news, subscribe to newsletters, and follow thought leaders on social media to keep up with the latest developments.

- **Twitter and LinkedIn**: Follow cybersecurity professionals and organizations to gain insights and share knowledge.
- **Podcasts and Webinars**: Tune into cybersecurity podcasts and webinars to hear from experts and learn about emerging trends and technologies.

b. Join Professional Communities

Participating in professional communities can foster learning and networking opportunities. Consider joining:

- **Online Forums**: Platforms like Reddit, Stack Exchange, and various cybersecurity forums allow for discussions on topics and sharing of knowledge.
- **Professional Associations**: Join organizations like (ISC)², ISACA, or the Information Systems Security Association (ISSA) for networking, training, and access to resources.
- **Local Meetups**: Attend local meetups or conferences to connect with peers and learn from industry experts.

c. Practical Application

Applying your knowledge through practical experiences enhances retention and skill development:

- **Hands-on Labs**: Engage in hands-on labs or simulations offered by platforms like TryHackMe, Hack The Box, or Cybrary to practice skills in real-world scenarios.
- **Capture the Flag (CTF) Competitions**: Participate in CTF competitions to hone your problem-solving and technical skills in a competitive environment.
- **Home Labs**: Set up a home lab to experiment with various tools and techniques in a controlled environment, allowing for hands-on learning and exploration.

Building a personal library of cybersecurity knowledge is an essential investment for any threat hunter or cybersecurity professional. By identifying key resources, organizing your library effectively, and committing to continuous learning and engagement, you can enhance your skills and adapt to the dynamic threat landscape. As the cybersecurity field continues to evolve, maintaining a proactive approach to knowledge acquisition and application will be key to success in protecting organizations against cyber threats. A well-rounded personal library not only empowers individual growth but also contributes to a more secure digital environment overall.

12.3 Networking Opportunities: Conferences and Meetups

In the fast-paced world of cybersecurity, building a professional network is crucial for career development, knowledge sharing, and staying updated on the latest trends and threats. Conferences and meetups provide excellent opportunities for threat hunters and cybersecurity professionals to connect, learn, and grow within the industry. This chapter explores the importance of networking, highlights key conferences and meetups, and offers tips for maximizing your networking experience.

1. The Importance of Networking in Cybersecurity

a. Knowledge Sharing and Learning

Networking with peers and industry leaders facilitates knowledge sharing, allowing professionals to learn from each other's experiences and insights. Engaging with others can provide different perspectives on cybersecurity challenges, methodologies, and technologies.

b. Career Development

Building a robust professional network can open doors to new career opportunities, mentorships, and collaborations. Many job openings are filled through referrals, and networking can increase your chances of being noticed by potential employers or partners.

c. Staying Informed on Industry Trends

Conferences and meetups often feature keynote speakers, panel discussions, and workshops that highlight the latest trends, threats, and solutions in cybersecurity. Engaging with industry experts and peers can help you stay informed about emerging technologies and best practices.

2. Key Conferences in Cybersecurity

a. DEF CON

Overview: DEF CON is one of the largest and most well-known hacker conventions, attracting security professionals, researchers, and enthusiasts from around the world. Held annually in Las Vegas, DEF CON features a wide range of talks, workshops, and hands-on activities.

Why Attend: Attending DEF CON offers an unparalleled opportunity to learn from leading experts, participate in discussions on cutting-edge topics, and network with a diverse group of attendees.

b. Black Hat

Overview: Black Hat is a premier cybersecurity conference that occurs annually in multiple locations, including Las Vegas, Europe, and Asia. The conference features high-level briefings and training sessions led by industry leaders and security researchers.

Why Attend: Black Hat is an ideal venue for professionals seeking advanced knowledge and insights into emerging threats and security technologies. Networking with speakers and attendees can lead to valuable connections and collaborations.

c. RSA Conference

Overview: The RSA Conference is one of the largest cybersecurity conferences globally, attracting thousands of professionals from various sectors. It features keynote speakers, panel discussions, and a vast exhibition showcasing the latest security products and services.

Why Attend: The RSA Conference offers a diverse range of topics, making it suitable for professionals at all levels. Networking opportunities abound, allowing attendees to connect with industry leaders, vendors, and peers.

d. SANS Institute Events

Overview: The SANS Institute hosts numerous training events, summits, and workshops worldwide, focusing on various cybersecurity topics. These events often feature hands-on training and certification opportunities.

Why Attend: SANS events are an excellent way to gain practical skills, meet industry experts, and network with fellow attendees who share similar interests and goals.

3. Local Meetups and Community Events

a. Local Security Meetups

Overview: Many cities host local cybersecurity meetups where professionals gather to discuss topics, share experiences, and network. These meetups often feature guest speakers, panel discussions, and informal networking sessions.

Why Attend: Local meetups provide a more intimate setting for networking and learning, making it easier to connect with fellow professionals in your area. They can also serve as a platform for discussing local threats and challenges.

b. OWASP Chapters

Overview: The Open Web Application Security Project (OWASP) has chapters worldwide that focus on improving software security. OWASP meetings often include presentations, workshops, and discussions on current security topics.

Why Attend: Joining an OWASP chapter provides access to a community of developers, security professionals, and enthusiasts dedicated to enhancing security practices. It's a valuable opportunity for knowledge sharing and networking.

c. Cybersecurity Hackathons

Overview: Hackathons focused on cybersecurity allow participants to collaborate on projects, develop skills, and solve challenges in a competitive environment. These events often attract diverse teams from various backgrounds.

Why Attend: Hackathons provide an excellent opportunity to meet like-minded individuals, showcase your skills, and work on real-world challenges. Networking at hackathons can lead to potential collaborations or job opportunities.

4. Tips for Maximizing Networking Opportunities

a. Prepare in Advance

Before attending a conference or meetup, research the event schedule, speakers, and attendees. Identify specific individuals or organizations you want to connect with and prepare thoughtful questions to engage them in conversation.